# Collins

## INTERNATIONAL PRIMARY ENGLISH
### AS A SECOND LANGUAGE

# Workbook 3

# HarperCollins
## PUBLISHERS
### Since 1817

William Collins' dream of knowledge for all began with the publication of his first book in 1819.
A self-educated mill worker, he not only enriched millions of lives, but also founded a flourishing publishing house. Today, staying true to this spirit, Collins books are packed with inspiration, innovation and practical expertise. They place you at the centre of a world of possibility and give you exactly what you need to explore it.

Collins. Freedom to teach.

An imprint of HarperCollins*Publishers*
The News Building
1 London Bridge Street
London SE1 9GF

browse the complete Collins catalogue at
www.collins.co.uk

© HarperCollins*Publishers* Limited 2017

10 9 8 7 6 5 4 3 2 1

ISBN 978-0-00-821365-7
Jennifer Martin asserts her moral right to be identified as the author of this work.

All rights reserved. No part of this publication may be reproduced, stored in a retrieval system, or transmitted in any form by any means, electronic, mechanical, photocopying, recording or otherwise, without the prior written permission of the Publisher or a licence permitting restricted copying in the United Kingdom issues by the Copyright Licensing Agency Ltd., 90 Tottenham Court Road, London W1T 4LP.

British Library Cataloguing in Publication Data

A catalogue record for this publication is available from the British Library.

Publisher Celia Wigley
Commissioning editor Karen Jamieson
Series editor Karen Morrison
Editor Alexander Rutherford
Project managed by Tara Alner
Edited by Cassandra Fox and Karen Williams
Proofread by Zoe Smith
Cover design by ink-tank and associates
Cover artwork by QBS Learning
Typesetting by QBS Learning
Illustrations by QBS Learning
Production by Lauren Crisp

Printed and bound by Grafica Veneta S. P. A.

**MIX**
Paper from responsible sources
FSC C007454
www.fsc.org

FSC™ is a non-profit international organisation established to promote the responsible management of the world's forests. Products carrying the FSC label are independently certified to assure consumers that they come from forests that are managed to meet the social, economic and ecological needs of present and future generations, and other controlled sources.

Find out more about HarperCollins and the environment at
www.harpercollins.co.uk/green

All exam-style questions, sample answers and mark schemes have been written by the authors.

**Acknowledgements**
The publishers gratefully acknowledge the permissions granted to reproduce copyright material in the book. Every effort has been made to contact the holders of copyright material, but if any have been inadvertently overlooked, the Publisher will be pleased to make the necessary arrangements at the first opportunity.

HarperCollins*Publishers* Limited for extracts and artwork from:
*Brown Bear and Wilbur Wolf* by Sarah Parry, illustrated by Judy Musselle, text © 2012 Sarah Parry. *Too Hot to Stop!* by Stephen Webb, illustrated by Stephen Webb, text © 2010 Stephen Webb. *Let's Go To Mars!* by Janice Marriott, illustrated by Mark Ruffle, text © 2005 Janice Marriott. *Hector and the Cello* by Ros Asquith, illustrated by Ros Asquith, text © 2005 Ros Asquith. *The Brave Baby* by Malachy Doyle, illustrated by Richard Johnson, text © 2004 Malachy Doyle. *Hansel and Gretel* by Malachy Doyle, illustrated by Tim Archbold, text © 2006 Malachy Doyle. *Living Dinosaurs* by Jonathan Scott and Angela Scott, illustrated by Jonathan Scott and Angela Scott, text © 2007 Jonathan Scott and Angela Scott. *Captain Scott: Journey to the South Pole* by Adrian Bradbury, text © 2012 Adrian Bradbury.

**Photo acknowledgements**
The publishers wish to thank the following for permission to reproduce photographs. Every effort has been made to trace copyright holders and to obtain their permission for the use of copyright materials. The publishers will gladly receive any information enabling them to rectify any error or omission at the first opportunity.

(t = top, c = centre, b = bottom, r = right, l = left)

Cover & p1 QBS Learning

p6t Nature Art/Shutterstock, p6tc Catmando/Shutterstock, p6c Aleksandar Grozdanovski, p6bc Eric Isselee/Shutterstock, p6bc Andrey Burmakin/Shutterstock, p17 Pyty/Shutterstock, p66tr Alexandr Junek Imaging/Shutterstock, p73b Corbis/Galen Rowell, p85 Macrovector/Shutterstock, p88 (mars) NASA/USGS, p88 (sun) NASA/SOHO, p93 Oleg Golovnev/Shutterstock, p95 Basheera Designs/Shutterstock, p119 (seasnake) poorbike/Shutterstock, p125t schankz/Shutterstock, p125tc WeStudio/Shutterstock, p125bc Rosa Jay/Shutterstock, p125b Anup Shah/Nature PL, p127 Jonathan and Angela Scott, p127bl praphab louilarpprasert/Shutterstock, p134 pavalena/Shutterstock, p135t Grobler du Preez/Alamy, p138 aodaodaodaod/Shutterstock, p144l Embleton, Ron (1930-88)/Private Collection/© Look and Learn/Bridgeman Images, p144r Mary Evans Picture Library, p145l Bibliotheque Nationale, Paris, France/Archives Charmet/Bridgeman Images, p145r Private Collection/© Look and Learn/Illustrated Papers Collection/Bridgeman Image, p147tl & bl NotionPic/Shutterstock, p147 Anastasia Boiko/Shutterstock, p151 Kate Evans and Bob Moulder

# Contents

1 **My world**
   Unit A   My family and friends   4
   Unit B   My neighbourhood   8
   Unit C   My school   9

2 **Special days**
   Unit A   Traditions around the world   12
   Unit B   Fun times   20
   Unit C   Party plans   25

3 **Animal stories**
   Unit A   Helping baby elephants   32
   Unit B   Swimming with dolphins   37
   Unit C   Brown Bear and Wilbur Wolf   42

4 **Wings and things**
   Unit A   Birds   45
   Unit B   Fly like a bird   50
   Unit C   Fly facts   57

5 **Adventures in different places**
   Unit A   Too hot to stop   63
   Unit B   Racing in a city   69
   Unit C   In Antarctica   72

6 **Space**
   Unit A   The Solar System   79
   Unit B   Let's Go to Mars!   86
   Unit C   Believe it or not!   93

7 **Storytime**
   Unit A   Hector and the Cello   100
   Unit B   The Brave Baby   104
   Unit C   Hansel and Gretel   110

8 **Interesting animals**
   Unit A   Don't touch!   118
   Unit B   Living dinosaurs   124
   Unit C   Big, bigger, the biggest   134

9 **Let's explore**
   Unit A   Marco Polo   143
   Unit B   Captain Scott   147
   Unit C   Amelia Earhart   155

# Topic 1  My world

## Unit A  My family and friends

**1  Fill in the information about yourself.**

My name is _____.

My surname is _____.

I am _____ years old.

My home address is: _____
_____
_____

My Photo

My favourite _____ is _____.

My favourite _____ is _____.

My favourite _____ is _____.

**2  Answer the questions about the Chan family.**

**a)** What job does King Fai Chan have?

He is a _____.

**b)** How old is Lee's sister?

She is _____ years old.

**c)** True or false?

Lee's sister is called Sandy. _____

Meg does not like swimming. _____

**d)** Who likes playing with their toes?

_____ likes playing with his toes.

Give personal information.

3 **Circle 'yes' or 'no'.**

a) Chad is a boy.      yes     no
b) Marie is a boy.      yes     no
c) Chad is shorter than Marie.      yes     no
d) Marie is the youngest child.      yes     no
e) Sheena is taller than Nish.      yes     no
f) Chad is taller than Marie.      yes     no
g) Sheena is the tallest girl.      yes     no

Chad      Nish      Sheena      Marie

Understand question words; use comparative and superlative adjectives.

**4  Are you taller or shorter than your partner? Fill in the missing word and your partner's name.**

I am _____ than _____.

**5  Fill in the information about your own family.**

_____ is the tallest person in my family.

_____ is the youngest person in my family.

**6  Draw a line to match each animal to a word that best describes it. One has been done for you.**

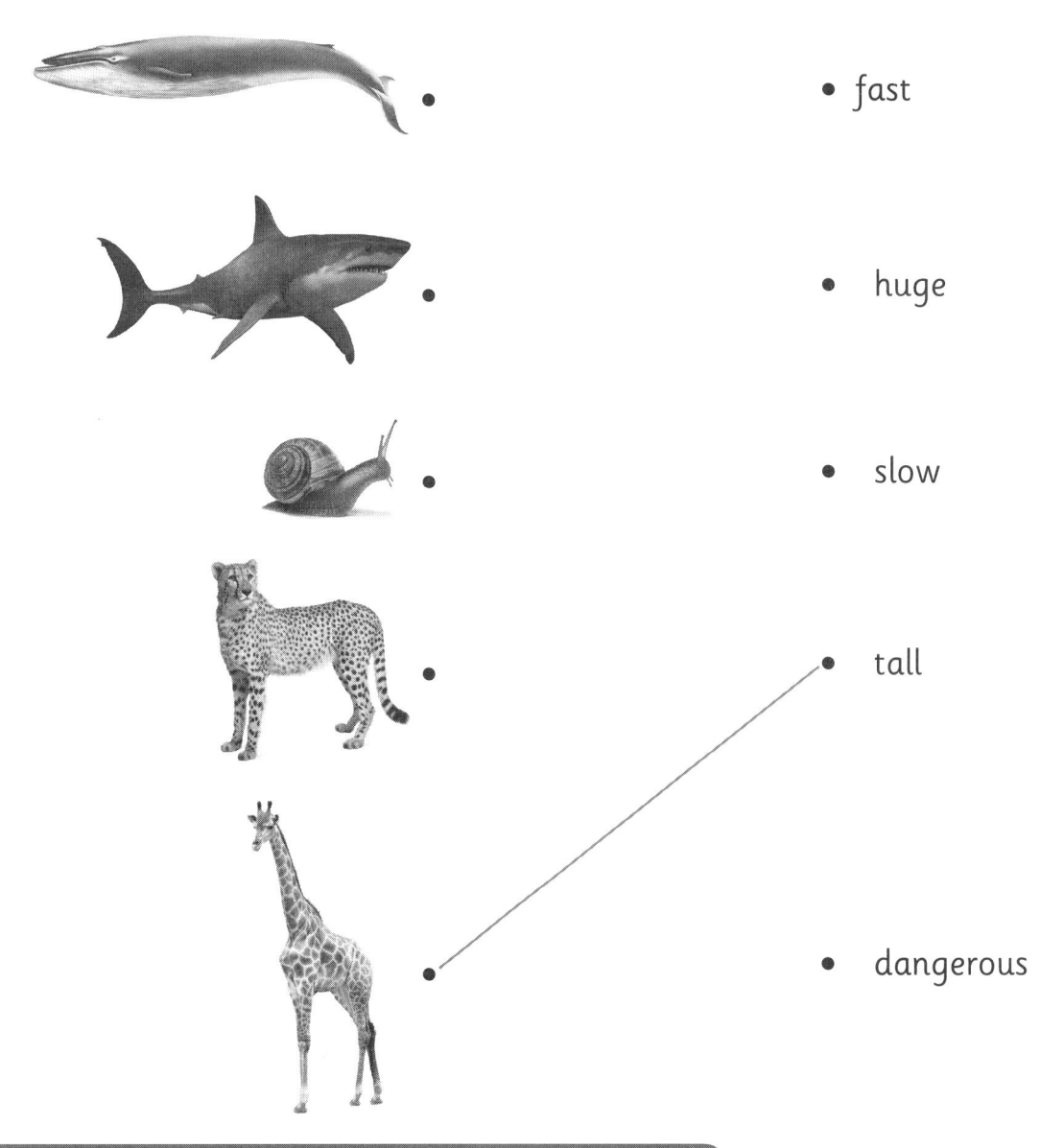

- fast
- huge
- slow
- tall
- dangerous

Use comparative and superlative adjectives.

**7** **Animals have families too and the members have different names. Complete the table. Use words from the box and check in a dictionary if you need to.**

> bull    chick    cub    doe    kitten    tom

| Animal | Mother | Father | Young |
|---|---|---|---|
| deer |  | stag | fawn |
| elephant | cow |  | calf |
| lion | lioness | lion |  |
| chicken | hen | rooster |  |
| cat | queen |  |  |

**8** **Fill in the missing words to compare the sizes of different animals.**

  **a)** A cub is small, a kitten is _____, but a chick is the _____.

  **b)** A doe is big, a lioness is _____, but a cow is the _____.

  **c)** A cat is strong, a lion is _____, but an elephant is the _____.

Use nouns; use comparative and superlative adjectives.

# Unit B  My neighbourhood

**1** **The pictures of the story are mixed up. Number them to show the correct order.**

☐ The town mouse knocked on the door.

☐ There was so much good food to eat!

☐ The town mouse was so disappointed with the meal he was served.

☐ Watch out! There's a cat!

☐ The town mouse invited the country mouse to join him.

☐ I'm going home where I can eat in peace.

**2** **Do you think the country mouse will visit the town mouse again? Why?**

_____

**3** **Think about this question.**

> Imagine that you are the country mouse. The town mouse invites you for another meal. What will you say to him?

Understand simple story; answer questions.

# Unit C  My school

1   **Can you find these items hidden in the picture?
Circle them as you find them.**

| board | bookcase | computer | desk | dictionary |
| eraser | glue | keyboard | map | mouse | pen |
| pencil | ruler | scissors | sentence | teacher |

I walk in the garden.

Diction

Extend basic vocabulary.

## 2 Read the questions. Circle the correct words to complete the answer.

a) Why did you eat the apple?

I ate the apple because I (was / is) hungry.

b) Why did you open the window?

I opened the window because I (feel / felt) too hot.

c) Why did Susie write a letter?

Susie wrote a letter because she (wanted / is wanting) to send her friend a message.

d) When did you begin your task?

I (begun / began) my task yesterday.

e) What did Jerry bring to school?

Jerry (brought / bringed) a ball to school.

f) What picture did Eli draw?

Eli (drew / drawed) a picture of a car.

g) Where did you find the books?

I (finded / found) the books in the small cupboard.

h) Did the teacher forgive the class?

Yes, the teacher (forgived / forgave) the class.

i) Where did Fadi go after school?

Fadi (went / goed) home after school.

j) Did Fadi pay for a new ruler?

Yes, Fadi (paid / payed) for a new ruler.

**3** **Look at the classroom on pages 8–9 in the Student's Book. Fill in the correct number words.**

I see _____ learners.

I see _____ teacher.

I see _____ boys.

**4** **Use the clues to complete the crossword puzzle.**

### Across

4   The leader of the school.
9   We use this to research the internet.

### Down

1   We sit on this.
2   Your teacher writes on this.
3   One child, many _____.
5   We measure things with this.
6   We draw with this.
7   We use _____ to stick pictures in our exercise books.
8   We write with this.

# Topic 2  Special days

## Unit A  Traditions around the world

**1** Look at the picture. Complete the sentences with 'a' or 'an'.

　　a) I can see _____ dragon.
　　b) I can see _____ envelope.
　　c) I can see _____ lantern.

**2** Circle the correct word to complete the sentences.

The woman is holding (a / an) packet.

She is pointing at (the / these) dancing dragon.

(The / an) boys are having fun.

It is (that / an) exciting day.

It is (this / an) amazing sight.

The Chinese New Year is (a / an) happy festival.

**3** Write three sentences about a special festival.

　　1: _____
　　2: _____
　　3: _____

12  Use determiners; write simple sentences.

**4  Choose words from the box to complete the sentences about Diwali.**

> colourful   decorate   diyas   fireworks   gifts
> gold   houses   noises   petals   rangolis

Another tradition that is part of Diwali is the lighting of _____. Diyas are oil lamps. People decorate their _____ with diyas and other bright lights. This shows that evil is chased away from the world. The world is no longer dark – it is filled with light.

During Diwali people buy each other _____. Some people buy clothes and others buy _____ jewellery.

During Diwali, people clean their houses and _____ the courtyards, walls and entrances with _____ rangolis. The _____ are made with coloured rice, dry flour, coloured sand or even flower _____.

Diwali celebrations are not complete without _____. Hindus believe that the loud _____ of the fireworks will scare evil away from their homes.

Understand detail; use determiners.   13

## 5  Circle the correct word in each sentence.

"I like (those / that) lantern," said Biyu.

"I think (this / those) are pretty!" exclaimed Biyu.

"I have decided to buy (that / these) lovely lanterns," said Biyu happily.

"It was difficult to choose which of (this / these) lanterns to buy," laughed Biyu.

**6   Read the poem about fireworks with a partner.**

BANG!
A ruby red star sparkles in the black sky
Up, up and up, higher than high,
A magical story, a very bright light
Come watch the fireworks with me tonight.

Brilliant blue bubbles, a shiny green glow
Fizzing explosions – Oh I love them so!
Just look at that rocket – see how it goes,
Where it will end up, nobody knows.

The fireworks float, they zoom and they blaze,
They make us so happy as upwards we gaze
Just look at the patterns that make the sky light –
We are so lucky to see them tonight!

*by Jennifer Martin*

**7   Read the poem again and answer these questions.**

a)   True or false?
     The fireworks sparkle in the sky. _____
     The fireworks make patterns in the sky. _____

b)   Write three pairs of rhyming words from the poem.

**c)** What colours are the different fireworks in the poem?

_____

**d)** How do we know the fireworks are being seen at night?

_____

_____

**e)** Complete these sentences.

I like fireworks because _____.

I don't like fireworks because _____.

I like fireworks, but _____.

I don't like fireworks, but _____.

**f)** Why do people have firework displays? List as many reasons as you can.

_____

_____

_____

_____

## 8 Think about these questions.

> Fireworks are used in celebrations all around the world.
>
> Some people think fireworks are dangerous. Do you agree with this? Give reasons for your answers.
>
> In some countries, fireworks may only be used in certain areas. Why do you think they have this rule?

9 **Find these countries in an atlas. Label them on the map.**

China
Turkey
Thailand
India

10 **Write a sentence about a festival celebrated in each country.**

China: _____
Turkey: _____
Thailand: _____
India: _____

Use proper nouns; describe places.

## 11 Write the correct word under each picture.

candle   diya   dragon   fireworks
lantern   krathong   parade   rangoli

a) _____
b) _____
c) _____
d) _____

e) _____
f) _____
g) _____
h) _____

## 12 Complete these sentences.

a) _____ make loud noises and beautiful colours in the sky.

b) Children sing and dance together in a _____.

c) Dancing _____ are made from silk, paper and bamboo.

d) A _____ is a small oil lamp used during Diwali.

Use nouns; complete sentences.

13 **Fill in the table.**

| Festival | Where? | What happens? | What do people do? |
|---|---|---|---|
| Chinese New Year | | | |
| Çocuk Bayrami | | | |
| Loy Krathong | | | |
| Diwali | | | |

# Unit B  Fun times

**1  Look at the picture. Complete the activities.**

Which cake has a candle on it? Circle it.

Which present is under the table? Colour it.

Find the balloon that is behind the table. Draw an X on it.

**2  Underline the sentence that is correct in each pair. Circle the word that is incorrect in the other sentence.**

a)  The present is in the table.        The present is on the table.

b)  The boy looked at the presents.     The boy looked with the presents.

c)  The girl played at the balloons.    The girl played with the balloons.

Understand and follow instructions; use prepositions.

## 3 Cross out the incorrect word in each sentence.

a) Willem has (many / much) friends.
b) He had (lots / most) of fun at his party.
c) The children made (some / many) noise.
d) There were (some / much) snacks to eat.
e) The balloons made (some / many) noise when they popped.
f) Some children felt a (little / some) shy at the party.
g) Bonnie didn't know (many / little) people at the party.

## 4 Read the sentences. Are they facts or opinions? Circle the correct word.

a) Willem had a birthday party.                         fact    opinion
b) Willem had the best birthday party ever.             fact    opinion
c) There was lots of food to eat.                       fact    opinion
d) It was the best party in the world.                  fact    opinion
e) Everybody should go to parties.                      fact    opinion
f) There should be balloons at parties.                 fact    opinion
g) Only boys should go to parties.                      fact    opinion
h) Boys and girls should go to the same parties.        fact    opinion
i) The children played games at the party.              fact    opinion
j) The party ended after three hours.                   fact    opinion

Use 'many/much'; recognise facts and opinions.

**5   Read the instructions and add to these pictures.**

Draw a candle on the cake.

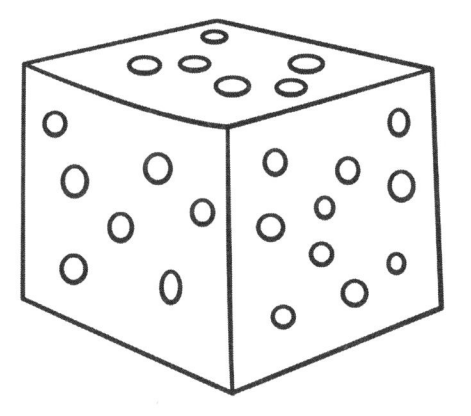

Draw a ribbon and a bow on the gift.

Draw two straws in the glass of juice.

Read and follow instructions.

**6** **Look at the pictures. Where is the cat? Write sentences using 'in', 'under' or 'in front of'.**

Use prepositions of location.

**7** **Complete this invitation for a party. Decorate it to show the type of party you are having.**

Dear _____

You are invited to my _____ party!

Date: _____
Place: _____
Time: _____

Please let me know if you can make it.
From: _____

# Unit C Party plans

1 **Use this sheet to plan a party for the twins, Kofi and Karl.**

Possible themes

Food and drink

Place

Games and activities

Decorations

Date and time

Clothing

Plan and write sentences.

**2** The pictures show what ingredients you need to bake a choc-chip birthday cake. Use the information to complete the list of ingredients.

| Ingredients for a choc-chip cake | What I'd need for two cakes |
|---|---|
| _____ eggs | |
| 1½ teaspoons of _____ | |
| _____ choc-chips | |
| _____ butter | |
| 2 cups of _____ | |
| 1 cup of _____ | |
| _____ of milk | |

26 Use numbers.

**3** **Use words from the box to complete the instructions for making the icing for the cake.**

> add    mix    pour    put    spread

**To make icing you will need:**
- A mixing bowl
- A wooden spoon
- 1 cup of icing sugar
- 1 teaspoon of cocoa powder
- ½ cup of hot water
- Two cups of soft margarine

**Instructions**:

First _____ the icing sugar and cocoa powder into the mixing bowl.

Next _____ the margarine.

_____ in the hot water.

Then _____ the ingredients with the wooden spoon until you have a smooth paste.

Finally, _____ the icing evenly onto the cake.

Use adverbs of sequence; imperative forms.

**4** **The instructions to make jelly boats are jumbled. Number them to show the correct order. Three instructions have been numbered for you.**

☐ Stir the mixture with a spoon until the jelly powder has dissolved.

☐ Carefully scoop out the fruit. Place the fruit in a small dish. Do not break the skin of the orange.

☐ Serve and enjoy.

☐ When the jelly has set, decorate the orange boats with the flags.

☐ Add the packet of jelly powder to the water.

| 2 | Boil the water.

☐ Carefully pour the jelly liquid into the orange peel halves.

☐ Place an orange on the chopping board. Cut it in half. Do this to all the oranges.

☐ Gently put the orange peel halves into the fridge for an hour.

| 1 | Wash your hands.

☐ While the jelly sets, make small flags out of paper and toothpicks.

| 3 | Pour 250 ml of boiling water into the mixing bowl.

Use adverbs of sequence; imperative forms.

5   Choose the correct word or words in each sentence. The picture will help you.

**a)** There are (a few / many) eggs.

**b)** There is (a lot / not a lot) of milk left over.

**c)** There are (a few / many) tablespoons.

**d)** There are (not a lot of / many) bags of sugar.

**e)** There is (some / none) milk.

6   **Write three sentences about the picture.**

1: _____

2: _____

3: _____

Use quantifiers; write simple sentences.

## 7 Circle the mistakes in this story.

Lucas was on a rush. He had to bake a cake, but he did not have enough ingredients. He went to the shop to buy what he needed.

Lucas put a bottle of milk around the basket. He also needed to flour and a butter. When he got home, he started to bake the cake.

He first switched off the oven. Then he mixed the eggs, butter and sugar apart. Lastly he added the milk or flour. He poured the batter on the baking tin and put it on the oven.

After 25 hours, Lucas carefully took the cake about the oven …

## 8 Rewrite the story correctly.

9  Micah asked his friends what food they would like to eat at a party. Use the information he collected to answer the questions.

|  | Snack 1: rotis | Snack 2: samosas | Snack 3: chocolate cake | Snack 4: ice cream |
|---|---|---|---|---|
| Children | 7 | 4 | 11 | 12 |

a) How many children want to eat chocolate cake? _____

b) How many children want to eat samosas? _____

c) How many children want to eat rotis? _____

d) How many children want to eat ice cream? _____

e) Which snack would you choose? _____

10 Draw a bar graph to show the information clearly.

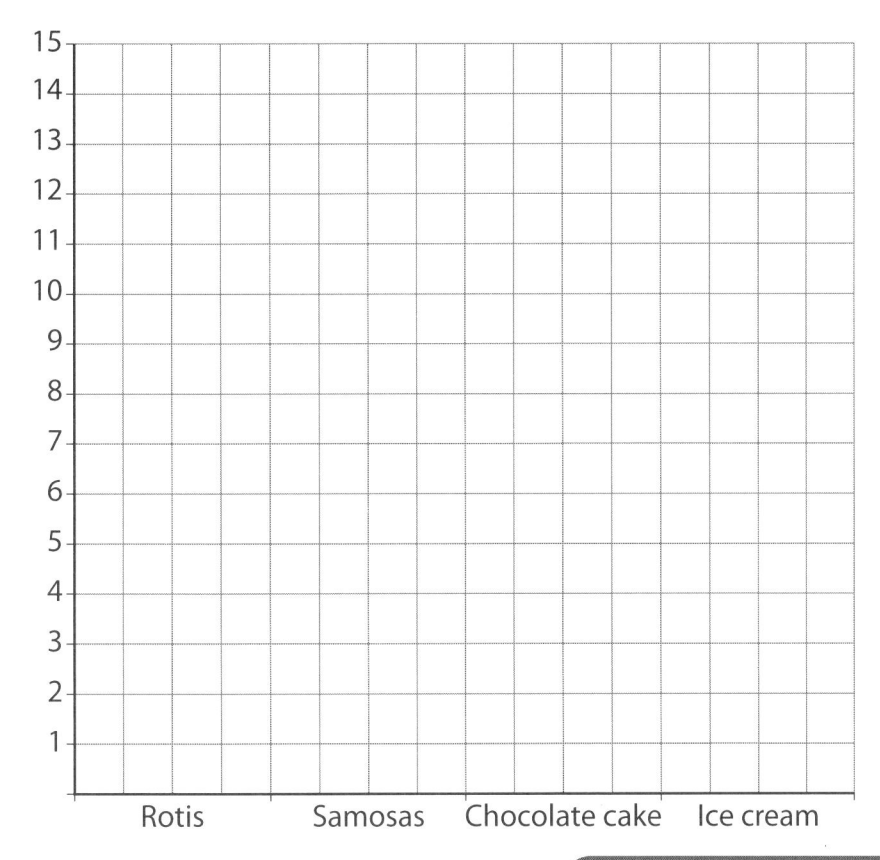

Use numbers; follow instructions.

# Topic 3  Animal stories

## Unit A  Helping baby elephants

**1  Answer 'true' or 'false' and correct the false sentences.**

a) Elephants eat plants.   true / false

_____

b) Elephants are brown and furry.   true / false

_____

c) Elephants have very small ears.   true / false

_____

d) Elephants are domestic animals.   true / false

_____

**2  Match each word in the box to the correct meaning.**

| African elephant  bull  calf  cow  herd  ivory  orphan  trunk |
|---|

| Word | Meaning |
|---|---|
|  | The name for an adult male elephant |
|  | The name for a baby elephant. |
|  | The name for an adult female elephant. |
|  | Elephants with large ears found in Africa. |
|  | A group of elephants. |
|  | A young animal with no parents. |
|  | Elephant tusks are made of this white material. |
|  | An elephant's nose. |

Understand detail; extend vocabulary.

**3** **Use the pictures on pages 16–17 in the Student's Book to find the answers to these questions.**

a) What is the calf drinking?
   _____

b) Who is the keeper feeding?
   _____

c) What is on the keeper's head?
   _____

d) What is the elephant eating?
   _____

e) Who is looking after the elephants?
   _____

**4** **The answers to two questions about elephants are given. Write what the question could have been.**

> They drink ten litres of milk a day for the first year of their lives.

> At night they get looked after by their keepers.

Answer and make up questions.

**5  Look at the pictures. Complete the sentences. Choose words from the box.**

| bath | drink | feed | play | sleep |

a)  The elephants like to _____ with the ball.
b)  The thirsty elephant likes to _____ milk.
c)  The elephants like to _____ in the mud.
d)  The elephant wants to _____ because he is tired.
e)  The keeper wants to _____ the hungry baby elephant.

**6  Listen and follow the instructions.**

34  Complete sentences; follow instructions.

**7** **Unscramble the words to make sentences.**

a) ball. elephants the chasing The blue are

_____

b) milk. baby drinking is elephant The

_____

c) walking are The elephants slowly. very

_____

d) baby lots fun. of elephants The are having

_____

e) calf. orphaned keeper feeding is the The elephant

_____

**8** **Unscramble the letters to spell each word correctly.**

_____  _____  _____
epalhnet            eprkee              uktss

9   **Pretend that you are a baby elephant. What do you like to do every day? Use the pictures to help you write some sentences to tell your keeper what you like to do. One sentence has been written for you as an example.**

I like _____.

10  **Write your own sentences about the words in the box. One sentence has been written for you as an example.**

| ears | elephants | eyes | grass | trunk | ~~tusks~~ |

The adult elephant has large tusks.

Write sentences with support.

## Unit B  Swimming with dolphins

1  **Label the parts of the dolphin. Use the words from the box.**

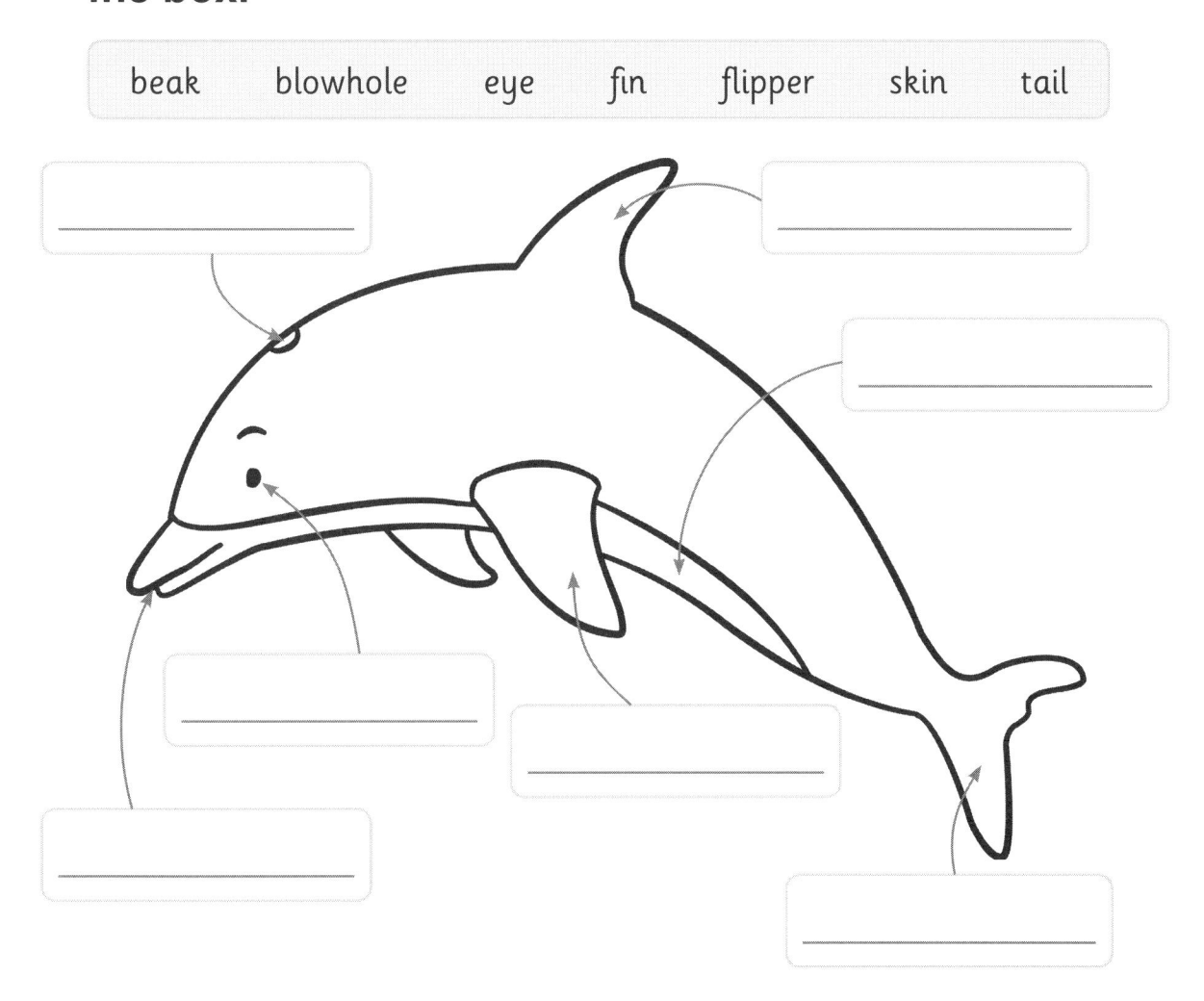

| beak | blowhole | eye | fin | flipper | skin | tail |

2  **Tick the words that describe the sounds a dolphin makes.**

☐ whistling   ☐ diving   ☐ squeaking

☐ clicking   ☐ rolling   ☐ calling

☐ roaring   ☐ beak   ☐ swimming

Use nouns; use adjectives.   37

**3  Circle the correct words in each sentence to complete the paragraphs.**

When Mom (tell / told) me I was (swimming / going to swim) with dolphins I (couldn't / can't) stop smiling. I'd (seen / saw) dolphins in the water near my home in New Zealand.

They were (dive / diving) and (rolling / roll) from side to side. I could hear them (squeak / squeaking) and (clicking / click).

I was (swam / swimming) free, just like them!

**4  Unscramble the sentences and rewrite them to match the story you heard.**

circling the sky. Sea birds in were

_____

water. in splashing Something was the

_____

put told wetsuit. She me to on a

_____

swam our towards boat. turned and The dolphins

_____

starting feel I was scared. bit a to

_____

**5  Number the sentences in the correct order (1–5) to match what happened in the story.**

☐ The dolphins swam around me leaping and playing.

☐ Mom and I walked down the jetty to the boat.

☐ I raised my hand and returned to the boat. My dream had come true.

☐ Cathy showed me a poster of the types of dolphins we might see.

☐ "Dolphins," I called. "They're dolphins!"

**6  Choose the correct ending for each sentence. Circle it.**

a) Dolphins live …           only in big lakes and rivers.
                             in oceans, seas and some rivers.

b) Dolphins use their blowhole for …   breathing.
                                       hearing.

c) Dolphins communicate by …   hunting and eating.
                               whistling and clicking.

d) Dolphins eat …            fish, squid, shrimps and octopus.
                             sea birds, orcas and fins.

e) One way to protect dolphins is to …   not swim with them.
                                         not put rubbish in the ocean.

f) When you swim with dolphins …   you need special equipment.
                                   you wear boots.

g) Dolphins can swim …       backwards.
                             very fast.

**7** **What do you know about dolphins? Write three complete sentences.**

    **a)** I know that dolphins can _____
_____.

    **b)** I know that they are able to _____
_____.

    **c)** I know that we have to _____
_____.

**8** **Complete these three sentences describing dolphins.**

    1: Dolphins are _____
_____.

    2: Dolphins have _____
_____.

    3: Dolphins are able to _____
_____.

**9** **Would you like to go swimming with dolphins? Fill in 'would' or 'wouldn't' below and complete the sentence.**

    I _____ like to go swimming with dolphins because
_____
_____.

Use 'I know'; write descriptions.

**10  Draw a line to match each question to its answer.**

Where do they live?  •  • Look after our seas and oceans. Don't put rubbish in the sea. Stop overfishing.

What do they eat?  •  • Dolphins make whistling and clicking sounds, then wait to see if the sound bounces back off an object. Sometimes they slap their tails or touch each other.

How fast can they swim?  •  • All over the world, in oceans and seas. Some even live in rivers.

How do they communicate?  •  • A male dolphin can live for 25 to 30 years. A female can live for 50 years.

How long do they live?  •  • They are carnivores. They hunt in groups to catch fish, squid, shrimps and octopus.

How can we help to protect dolphins?  •  • Up to 40 km per hour.

**11  Write four sentences of your own about dolphins.**

1: _____

_____

2: _____

_____

3: _____

_____

4: _____

_____

Answer questions; write sentences.

# Unit C  Brown Bear and Wilbur Wolf

1  **Fill in the missing letters in each word from the story. Then draw lines to match the words to the pictures.**

a) b _ _ _

b) w _ l _

c) f _ _ h

d) b _ r _

e) b e _ _ e r

f) d _ _ r

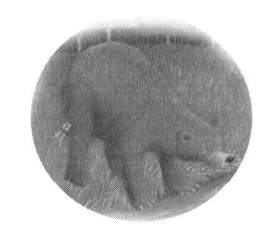

2  **Label the places shown in the picture. Choose words from the box.**

| forest | meadow | mountain | river | valley |

Spell familiar words; extend vocabulary.

**3** **How is each character feeling in the picture? Choose words from the box.**

| lonely | scared | strong | weak |

**4** **Write 'true' or 'false' next to each sentence.**

a) Brown Bear lost his sense of smell. _____

b) The birds, beaver and deer helped Brown Bear to catch food. _____

c) Brown Bear tried to eat the deer, the birds and the beaver. _____

d) Wilbur Wolf was too old and weak to catch food. _____

e) Brown Bear was hungry and lonely until he met Wilbur Wolf. _____

**5** **Answer these questions with complete sentences.**

a) How do you help your friends? _____

b) How do your friends help you? _____

c) What did you like most about this story? _____

Use adjectives; identify facts; answer questions.

**6** **Think of words to fill in the table. Use the example to help you.**

| Characters | Words to show we don't like the character | Words to show that we don't mind the character | Words to show that we do like the character |
|---|---|---|---|
| Brown Bear | mean, sneaky | large, hairy | kind, brave |
| Wilbur Wolf | | | |
| The beaver | | | |
| The birds | | | |
| The deer | | | |

# Topic 4 Wings and things

## Unit A  Birds

1  **Label the diagram. Choose words from the box.**

| beak | claws | eyes | feathers | feet |
| head | legs | neck | tail | wings |

Extend vocabulary.

**2** **Match each bird to its name. Unscramble the letters and write the name of each bird.**

> crow    hawk    heron    ostrich    parrot
> peacock    puffin    seagull    woodpecker

a) tri<u>o</u>sch _____

b) accekop _____

c) rone<u>h</u> _____

d) dopeo<u>w</u>kcre _____

e) wo<u>c</u>r _____

f) kwa<u>h</u> _____

g) tro<u>p</u>ar _____

h) niffu<u>p</u> _____

i) glluе<u>s</u>a _____

**3** **Choose the three birds you like best. Complete the sentences.**

I like the _____ best. I also like the _____ and the _____ .

Extend vocabulary; express opinions.

4 **Answer these questions.**

   a) Which bird is the biggest? _____

   b) Is a seagull bigger than a peacock? _____

   c) Is a woodpecker bigger than a heron? _____

   d) Is a puffin smaller than a heron? _____

   e) Which bird is the smallest? _____

5 **Read the sentences. Write 'true' or 'false'.**

   a) An ostrich can fly. _____

   b) The ostrich is the biggest bird of all. _____

   c) Some birds can learn to talk. _____

   d) Woodpeckers eat things like crabs and prawns. _____

   e) Owls can fly silently. _____

6 **Complete the sentences below. Use the words from the box.**

   | bright | fruit | noisy | seeds | talk | tame |

   The parrot is a _____ bird.
   It has very _____ feathers.
   Parrots can be taught to _____.
   _____ parrots will not fly away.
   Parrots eat _____ and _____.

7 **Answer the question.**

   There are some goats and some birds in a field. If there are 14 heads and 36 legs, how many birds are there?

Find information; spell familiar words.

## 8 Circle the correct word in each sentence.

a) (A / An) owl catches a rat.
b) The (owl / owls) catch a mouse.
c) One (owl / owls) catches a mouse.
d) (A / An) hawk swoops down.
e) (The / An) hawks swoop down.
f) Many (hawk / hawks) swoop down.
g) (An / A) ostrich is a large bird.
h) (The / Many) ostrich is a large bird.
i) (Many / A) parrot made a noise.
j) (Much / Many) parrots make a lot of noise.

## 9 Read the information on pages 22–23 of the Student's Book again. Complete these fact files.

| Seagulls | Woodpeckers |
|---|---|
| Description: _____ | Description: _____ |
| Where they live: _____ | Where they live: _____ |
| What they eat: _____ | What they eat: _____ |
| **Ostriches** | **Parrots** |
| Description: _____ | Description: _____ |
| Where they live: _____ | Where they live: _____ |
| What they eat: _____ | What they eat: _____ |

Use determiners; find and use information.

**10** **These are the first two pages of a book about birds. Read the information and answer the questions.**

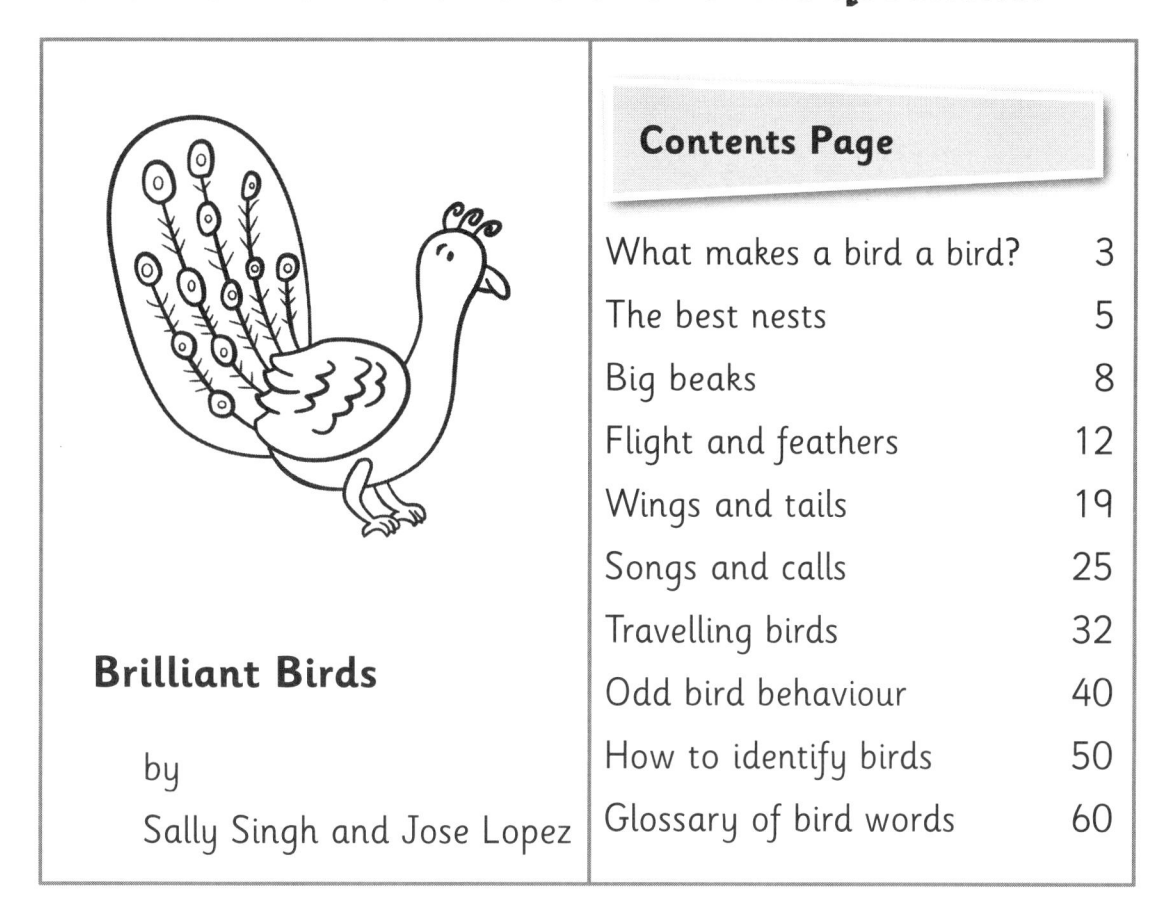

**Brilliant Birds**

by

Sally Singh and Jose Lopez

| Contents Page | |
|---|---|
| What makes a bird a bird? | 3 |
| The best nests | 5 |
| Big beaks | 8 |
| Flight and feathers | 12 |
| Wings and tails | 19 |
| Songs and calls | 25 |
| Travelling birds | 32 |
| Odd bird behaviour | 40 |
| How to identify birds | 50 |
| Glossary of bird words | 60 |

**a)** What is the name of the book? _____

**b)** Who wrote this book? _____

**c)** On which pages can you read about bird songs? _____

**d)** What can you read about on page 32? _____

**e)** Where would you look up the meaning of a word?
_____

**f)** How many pages have information about flight and feathers?
_____

**g)** Which chapter seems most interesting? Why? _____

Read for information; answer questions.  49

# Unit B Fly like a bird

## 1 Write the correct word next to each definition.

| aeroplane | bellyflying | brave | dangerous | free fall | grip |
| parachute | safe | scared | skydiver | steer | team |

_____ A flying vehicle with wings and an engine.

_____ To control the direction in which something is moving.

_____ A person who jumps from a plane and falls to the ground before opening a parachute.

_____ The time before a skydiver opens his or her parachute when they are falling quickly through the air.

_____ Something that could hurt you.

_____ Holding onto other skydivers as you free fall.

_____ A group of people who do a sport or activity together.

_____ A special way of holding onto something.

_____ Not too scared to do something.

_____ Frightened or nervous about something.

_____ Equipment used in skydiving. This is a large canopy that opens and lets the skydiver fall slowly and safely to the ground.

_____ Something that won't hurt you or do any damage.

## 2 Unscramble the letters and write the correct words.

riskeydv

pleeranoa

ctuhepraa

_____      _____      _____

Extend vocabulary.

**3** **Listen to the interview with a skydiver. Fill in the missing words.**

**Interviewer:** _____ you jump out of an aeroplane tomorrow?

**Skydiver:** Yes, I _____ definitely jump tomorrow.

**Interviewer:** What _____ you wear when you jump?

**Skydiver:** I _____ wear a parachute.

**Interviewer:** What _____ you do next week?

**Skydiver:** I _____ meet my friends for dinner.

**Interviewer:** How _____ you get to the restaurant?

**Skydiver:** I _____ drive my car.

**4** **Listen and follow the instructions.**

| 1 | 2 | 3 | 4 | 5 | 6 | 7 | 8 | 9 | 10 |
|---|---|---|---|---|---|---|---|---|---|
| 11 | 12 | 13 | 14 | 15 | 16 | 17 | 18 | 19 | 20 |
| 21 | 22 | 23 | 24 | 25 | 26 | 27 | 28 | 29 | 30 |
| 31 | 32 | 33 | 34 | 35 | 36 | 37 | 38 | 39 | 40 |
| 41 | 42 | 43 | 44 | 45 | 46 | 47 | 48 | 49 | 50 |
| 51 | 52 | 53 | 54 | 55 | 56 | 57 | 58 | 59 | 60 |
| 61 | 62 | 63 | 64 | 65 | 66 | 67 | 68 | 69 | 70 |
| 71 | 72 | 73 | 74 | 75 | 76 | 77 | 78 | 79 | 80 |
| 81 | 82 | 83 | 84 | 85 | 86 | 87 | 88 | 89 | 90 |
| 91 | 92 | 93 | 94 | 95 | 96 | 97 | 98 | 99 | 100 |

Use 'will/shall'; use numbers.

**5** **Use 'so', 'but' or 'because' to join each pair of sentences. Write the new sentence you make.**

a) Joe tripped when he landed. He didn't hurt himself.
_____

b) Tina was ill. She couldn't skydive.
_____

c) We went on a plane. We wanted to skydive.
_____

d) I needed a different helmet. That one was too big.
_____

e) It was cold in the plane. We didn't notice.
_____

f) It was a cloudy day. We couldn't see the ground.
_____

g) I couldn't hold onto Joe's hand. I had the wrong grip.
_____

**6** **Complete these sentences.**

a) I have never been to _____ but I would like to go there.

b) I have never eaten _____ but I would like to try it.

c) I have never travelled in a _____ but I would like to travel in one.

d) I have never seen a _____ but I would like to see one.

e) I have never drunk _____ but I would like to try it.

f) I have never played _____ but I would like to play it.

Use 'so', 'but', 'because'.

**7  Choose five sports that you think could be dangerous.**

- ice hockey
- soccer
- swimming
- running
- bowls
- cricket
- gymnastics
- cycling
- canoeing
- mountain biking
- bungee jumping
- hang gliding
- diving
- hiking
- horseback riding
- kitesurfing
- mountain climbing
- skydiving
- parkour
- rock-climbing
- roller skating
- windsurfing
- sailing
- scuba diving
- snorkeling
- skateboarding
- skiing
- surfing

Extend vocabulary.

8  **Rank the sports you circled from the most dangerous to the least dangerous.**

Most dangerous: _____

_____

_____

_____

Least dangerous: _____

9  **Complete this conversation using the sport you think is the most dangerous.**

**Franco:** What do you think about _____?

**Sophia:** I think people who _____ are _____.

**Franco:** Why do you think that?

**Sophia:** I think they are _____ because _____.

10  **Complete these sentences about the sport you think is the most dangerous.**

> I think it's the most dangerous because _____.
>
> I think I would _____.
>
> I also think _____.

Express opinions; use 'I think'.

**11  Read the poem.**

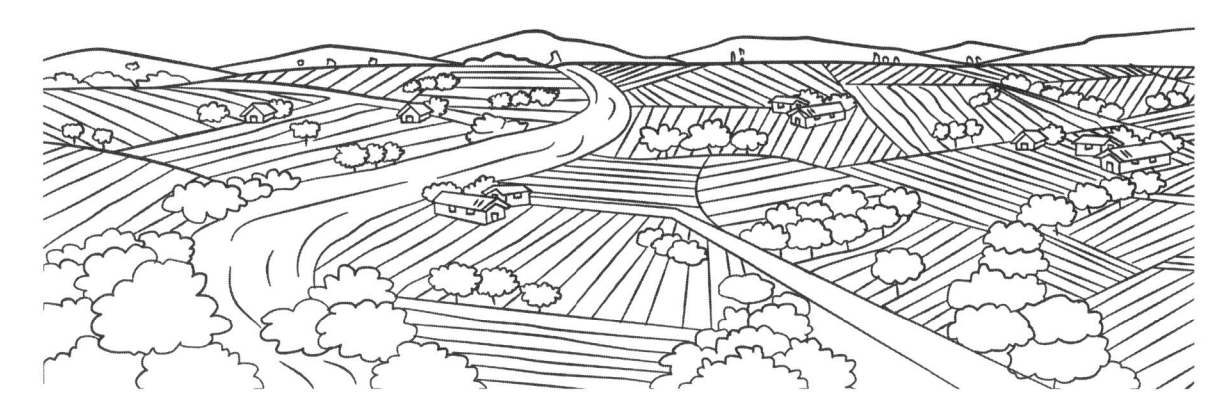

### I Want to Be a Bird

I want to be a bird with wings
To fly around and see new things
Like little goats on mountains high
I'd touch the clouds as they float by.

I want to be a bird that soars
And doesn't live behind closed doors
Who flies around from here to there
Enjoying life without a care.

Imagine seeing the world from high –
My home is in the bright blue sky
What are those dots? Where are the farms?
Oh see those children waving their arms!

But oh dear me, I'll have to dive
Out of a plane – will I survive?
Indeed I will – count 1, 2, 3
I'm like a bird, I'm flying free!

*by Jennifer Martin*

12 **Answer the questions about the poem.**

   a) Why does the poet want to be a bird?
   b) Why do the farms look like dots?
   c) What do these words mean?

   float: _____

   soars: _____

   dive: _____

   d) Is the poet really flying at the end of the poem? How do you know?

13 **Read the poem aloud again. Listen for the words that rhyme. Complete the table.**

| Word | Word in the poem that rhymes with this word | Another word that rhymes with this word |
|---|---|---|
| wings | | |
| high | | |
| soars | | |
| there | | |
| high | | |
| farms | | |
| dive | | |
| three | | |

Answer questions; identify rhyming words.

# Unit C  Fly facts

**1  Answer these questions about flies. Choose some of the words from the box.**

| a lot of    many    much    not many    one    six    ten    two |
|---|

a) How many legs does a fly have?

A fly has _____ legs.

b) How many hairs are on a fly's legs?

There are _____ hairs on a fly's legs.

c) How many eggs does a fly lay?

A fly lays _____ eggs.

d) How many wings does a fly have?

A fly has _____ wings.

e) How many flies have you seen in your life?

I have seen _____ flies in my life.

f) How many different types of flies are there?

There are _____ different types of flies.

**2  Circle the best word in each sentence.**

a) I have to chase flies off my (food / germs).

b) I (have / had) to chase away flies to prevent the spread of (food / germs).

c) Yesterday I (had / have) to chase flies off my table.

d) The rotten food (had / have) lots of flies on it.

e) Yesterday I had to chase away flies as they are (dirty / clean).

Use quantifiers; use 'had/have' correctly.

**3** **Unscramble the words to make sentences. Write the sentences on the lines.**

a) have chase to I flies away.

_____

b) I chase had yesterday to flies away.

_____

**4** **Tick the box that matches your opinion.**

|  | Agree | Disagree | Don't know |
|---|---|---|---|
| Birds should not be kept in cages. |  |  |  |
| Birds are better pets than cats. |  |  |  |
| Birds make the best pets. |  |  |  |
| You are sensible if you want to skydive. |  |  |  |
| It's fun to jump out of aeroplanes. |  |  |  |
| Skydiving is not dangerous. |  |  |  |
| Flies are a nuisance. |  |  |  |
| All flies should be destroyed. |  |  |  |
| Flies make good pets |  |  |  |

**5** **Read the sentences. Fill in the missing words using 'a', 'an' or 'some'.**

a) The fly wants to sit on _____ apple.

b) The fly is trying to sit on _____ food.

c) Would you like to eat _____ food?

d) I wouldn't like to be _____ fly.

e) I saw _____ flies on my food.

f) _____ baby fly is called a maggot.

Express opinions; use determiners.

**6** Answer these questions as if you are a large housefly being interviewed.

Why are your feet so dirty?

Is it true that you spit on your food?

What good things do you do?

What are your favourite foods?

**7** **Read the story and fill in the missing words with words from the box.**

| a    an    any    some    this |

Once upon a time there was _____ fly. But _____ fly was not like his friends. It was a very strange fly because it did not like germs.

He would not sit on _____ rotting food, even when he was hungry!

Even if there was _____ old food on a plate or _____ apple that was rotten, he would rather sit on a clean surface. What a strange fly!

**8** **Find the words in the box in the wordsearch and circle them. Then work with a partner. Take turns to test each other's spelling. Say a word from the box and check whether your partner can spell it.**

| ~~dirty~~ | germ | invisible | maggots | rotting | sticky | tiny | wings |

| i | n | v | i | s | i | b | l | e |
|---|---|---|---|---|---|---|---|---|
| d | u | c | n | t | i | n | y | s |
| i | a | l | g | g | e | r | m | t |
| r | c | e | w | i | n | g | s | i |
| t | i | v | l | e | h | i | i | c |
| y | m | a | g | g | o | t | s | k |
| e | t | r | y | p | c | t | t | y |
| r | o | t | t | i | n | g | s | r |

_____    _____

_____    _____

_____    _____

_____    _____

Extend vocabulary; build spelling skills. 61

**9  Choose the best word to join each pair of sentences. Write the new sentence.**

| and | because | but | so |

**a)** There were lots of flies.   We covered the food.

_____

**b)** We kept the window closed.   Some flies still got in.

_____

**c)** We couldn't eat the food.   It was covered with flies.

_____

**d)** Flies are pests.   Flies spread germs.

_____

**e)** Flies clean their legs.   Small pieces of food fall off.

_____

**f)** Flies don't have teeth.   They can't bite or chew.

_____

**g)** Most insects have four wings.   Flies only have two.

_____

Use conjunctions.

# Topic 5  Adventures in different places

## Unit A  Too hot to stop

1  **Draw lines to join pairs of rhyming words.**

sun • • track
tree • • parade
back • • begun
shade • • me
by • • pool
cool • • sky
dune • • side
wide • • soon

2  **The gazelle's name is Hoppitt because he hops and jumps around. Think of names for his friends. Write the names below each picture.**
**Tell your group why you chose these names.**

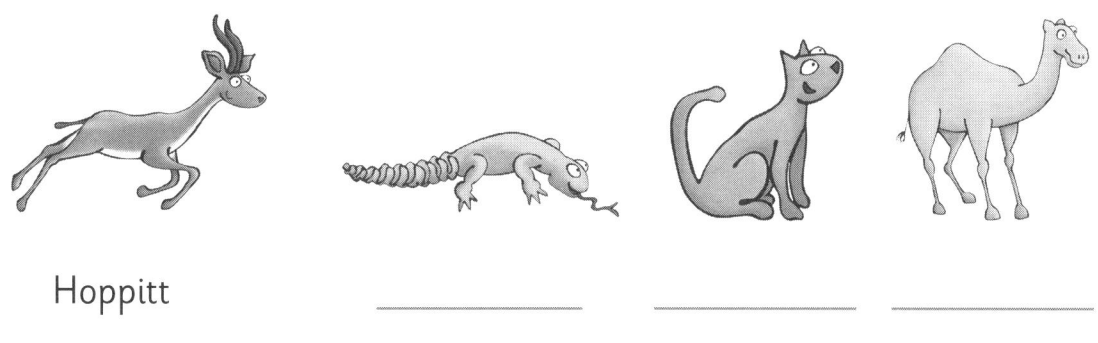

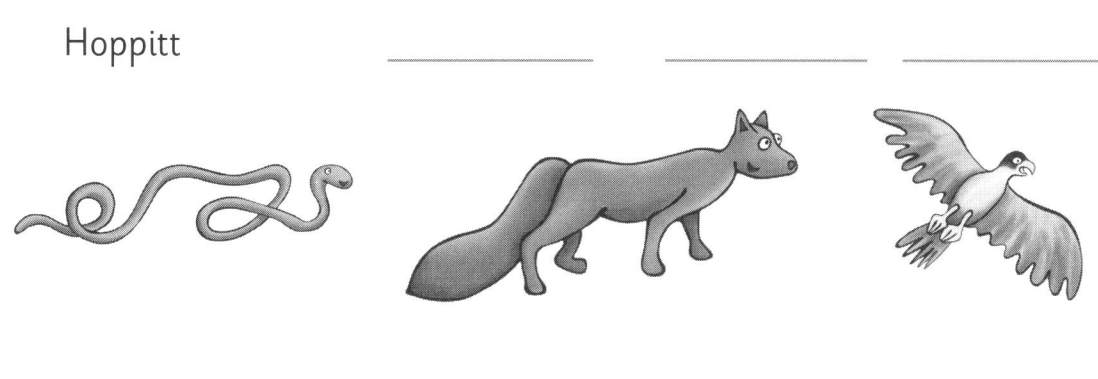

Hoppitt _____  _____  _____

_____  _____  _____

Identify rhyming words; use proper nouns.  63

3  **Number the sentences from 1 to 4 to match the order of the story.**

☐ "Stop it, Hoppitt, stop it," warned the falcon flying by.

☐ Hoppitt hopped over the sand dune and splashed into the desert pool.

☐ Hoppitt the Gazelle likes to hop, hop, hop!

☐ It was too hot for Hoppitt and his friends to stop.

4  **Look at the picture. Use words from the box to complete the sentences.**

| at | behind | between | in | into | next to |
| on | opposite | over | towards | under | |

a) The sand cat is sitting _____ a cactus.

b) The fox is standing _____ the rocks.

c) The falcon is flying _____ the sand dunes.

d) The gazelle is jumping _____ the cool water.

e) The snake is slithering _____ the cool water.

f) The lizard is standing _____ the shade.

Sequence story events; use prepositions.

5   **Use this table to help you make five sentences about the desert. Choose one part from each column to make each sentence.**

| There are a few | plants  | near the rocks.   |
| There is some   | stones  | in the desert.    |
| There are some  | trees   | on the ground.    |
| There are many  | shade   | growing there.    |
| There isn't much| rain    | to drink.         |
|                 | water   | under the bushes. |
|                 | animals |                   |

1: _____

2: _____

3: _____

4: _____

5: _____

6   **What could the animals be saying? Complete the conversation.**

**Camel:** It is so hot...

**Snake:** I wish...

**Sand cat:** I'm going to...

**Lizard:** I'll just...

Write sentences with support.

## 7 Read about sand cats. Answer the questions.

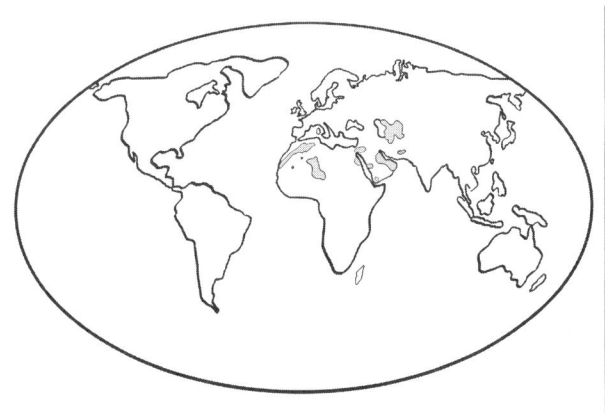

The sand cat is a wild cat that is about the same size as a pet cat. Sand cats weigh about 3.4 kilograms. They look like pet cats but they behave and sound like wild cats.

The sand cat likes to live in the sandy desert. Its sand coloured coat makes it hard to see against the sand and dry bushes. It has thick fur on its paws so that it can walk on very hot sand without getting burned. It also has very big ears which help it hear very well.

The sand cat does not need to drink water to live. It gets almost all the water it needs from the animals that it kills and eats. The sand cat hunts animals to eat at night. It eats small animals like lizards and birds.

a) Is a sand cat bigger or smaller than a pet cat?

b) How does a sand cat behave and sound?

c) Why is the sand cat difficult to see in the desert?

d) Why do you think it is called a 'sand cat'?

e) How is the sand cat well suited to living in the desert?

## 8 Write a good word to complete each sentence.

a) The sand cat can live in a desert _____ it has adapted to the heat.

b) The sand cat doesn't need to drink water to live _____ it gets enough from the prey it eats.

c) The snake likes the heat _____ it lies in the sun.

d) Hoppitt feels too hot _____ he jumps into the cool water.

e) The falcon told Hoppitt to 'stop it' _____ he could see a pool of water.

f) Hoppitt, sand cat, lizard _____ the camel were happy to jump into the water.

g) They were happy to jump into the water _____ they felt too hot.

## 9 Make up a good ending for each sentence. The first one has been done as an example.

a) A fish likes water, but *a cat does not.*

b) A sand cat eats lizards, but _____.

c) A camel lives in a desert, but _____.

d) A snake slithers, but _____.

e) A falcon flies high in the sky, but _____.

## 10 Name three animals that live in a desert.

_____    _____    _____

## 11 Circle the animal that does not fit in this group. Tell your partner why it doesn't fit.

cat          lion          tiger          bear

Use conjunctions; extend vocabulary.    67

**12** Circle the words in each row that must be written with capital letters. Write the words correctly on the lines at the end of the rows.

a) red   sahara desert   run   hurry _____

b) jump   hoppitt   hot   snake _____

c) middle east   shade   sand dune   sand _____

d) africa   camel   lizard   parade _____

**13** Rewrite each sentence correctly using capital letters, full stops or question marks.

a) have you seen hoppitt

_____

b) i saw him run past the lizard

_____

c) was hoppitt running very fast

_____

d) hoppitt was running as fast as the wind

_____

**14** Use these question words and make five questions that you could ask Hoppitt.

a) Where _____?

b) How _____?

c) What _____?

d) Why _____?

e) Who _____?

# Unit B  Racing in a city

1  **Complete the sentences using words from the box.**

| crew | co-driver | engine | helmet |
|---|---|---|---|
| route | rules | stage | support |

a) The route is navigated by the _____.

b) The car is repaired by the _____.

c) The driver must start the _____.

d) They must obey the _____.

e) You must always wear a _____.

f) Tomorrow they will complete a _____.

g) That is a dangerous _____.

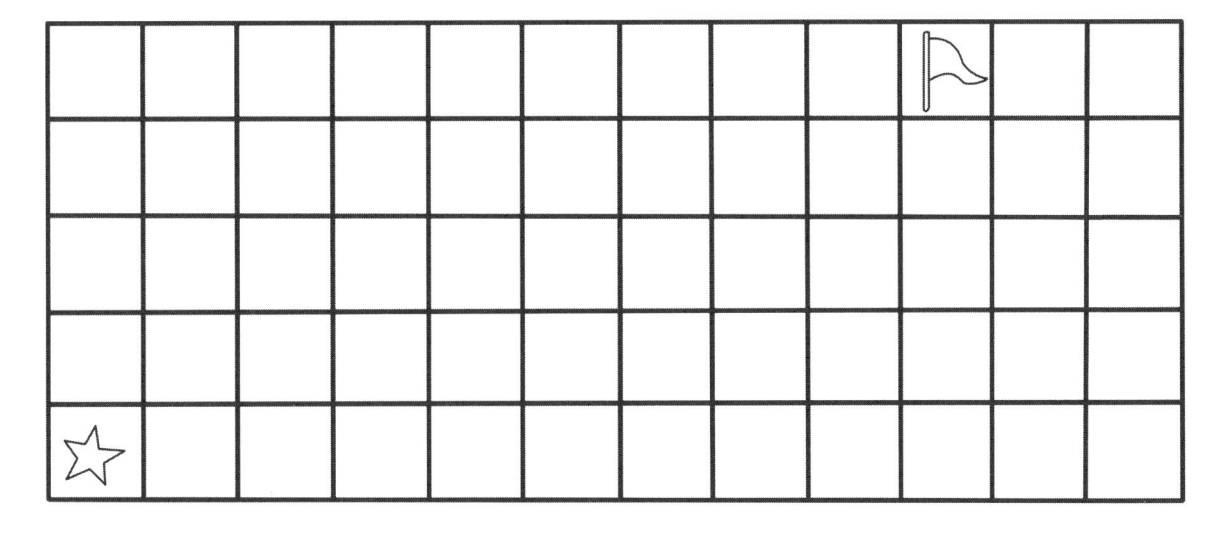

2  **Start at the star. Draw your own route on the grid. You may only move straight and turn left or right. Your route must end at the flag.**

Use a different colour to follow your partner's route.

Complete sentences; follow instructions.

**3** **What question could have been asked to give each answer? Write in your ideas.**

| Question | Answer |
|---|---|
|  | Rallying is a form of motorsport. |
|  | It takes place on public and private roads. |
|  | Yes, we're allowed to use both sides of the road. |
|  | We have to obey all the rules of the road on touring stages. |
|  | The Dunlop Targa Rally of New Zealand is six days long. |
|  | The co-driver has to be good at navigation. |

**4** **Complete the conversation below.**

**Vince:** The tyre is flat. Where is the jack?

**Hans:** I put _____ on the driver's seat.

**Vince:** Where _____ the pump?

**Hans:** I left _____ in the support car.

**Vince:** Have you seen the co-driver yet?

**Hans:** Yes, I saw her with the driver. She was talking to him.

**Vince:** What did she say to _____?

**Hans:** She said _____ could still win the rally.

**Vince:** Do _____ think we can win?

**Hans:** I certainly do!

## 5 Read the clues. Complete the crossword puzzle.

**Across**

1 The car that comes first is the _____
3 Part of a car that gives it power.
4 A part or section of a rally.
6 Direction or way to travel along a road.
7 A hard hat that protects your head.

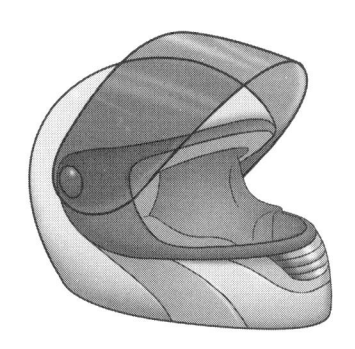

**Down**

2 Plan a route and follow it on a map.
4 Not in danger.
5 Instructions that tell us what we are allowed to do or not do.

# Unit C  In Antarctica

**1  Draw lines to match the words to their meanings.**

blubber • • a flap of skin on a penguin's tummy which folds down over an egg, keeping it warm

pouch • • big pieces of ice floating in the sea

glaciers • • tiny sea creatures that look like shrimps

icebergs • • an animal that gives birth to live babies and feeds its young with milk from the mother's body

krill • • rivers of ice that move very slowly downhill

mammal • • a layer of fat under the skin, which helps to keep some animals warm

orca • • another name for a Killer whale

**2  Look at the picture. Label the animals and then answer the questions.**

a) How many seals can you see? _____

b) How many penguins are there? _____

c) How many orcas are jumping out of the water? _____

Use nouns; numbers to count.

3  **Answer 'yes' or 'no'.**

   a) Is a penguin good at hopping? _____

   b) Is a seal good at running? _____

   c) Is a shark good at walking? _____

4  **What are seals good at? Circle the correct answer.**

   a) Seals are good at (diving / hopping).

   b) Seals are good at (walking / swimming).

   c) Seals are good at (diving / running).

5  **Listen as your teacher asks questions. Find the answers in the fact file.**

| Factfile: Antarctic penguins ||||
| Penguin | Weight | Height | Food |
| --- | --- | --- | --- |
| Rockhopper | 2–4 kg | 45–55 cm | mostly krill |
| Adelie | 4–5 kg | 70 cm | mostly krill |
| Chinstrap | 4–5 kg | 70–75 cm | mostly krill |
| Macaroni | 5–6 kg | 70 cm | mostly krill |
| Gentoo | 5–8 kg | 75–90 cm | fish and krill |
| King | 10–20 kg | 90 cm | fish and squid |
| Emperor | 20–40 kg | 120 cm | fish and squid |

Understand and find information and detail.

## 6 Complete the sentences. Choose words from the box.

| coldest | greatest | larger | largest | smallest | stronger | windiest |

a) Antarctica is the _____ and _____ place on Earth.

b) The ocean around Antarctica has _____ waves and _____ winds than anywhere else on Earth.

c) Rockhoppers are the _____ penguins.

d) Seals are the penguins' _____ enemy.

e) King penguins are _____ than Adelie penguins.

## 7 Write the names of the different types of penguins in alphabetical order.

_____  _____  _____  _____

_____  _____  _____

## 8 Answer these questions.

a) Which penguins do not eat krill? _____

b) Is the King penguin taller or shorter than the Rockhopper penguin?

_____

c) How much do the heaviest penguins weigh? _____

d) Are you taller or shorter than a King penguin? _____

e) How much taller are King penguins than Macaroni penguins?

_____

f) Which penguins can weigh more than 10 kilograms? _____

**9  Fill in the missing words from the poem.**

Penguins are good at _____.

Penguins swim fast in the _____.

Penguins are good at _____.

I wish they'd come play with _____!


They love to _____ in cold water,

They _____ for krill and for fish,

They look after their _____ so carefully,

Oh, would someone please grant me my _____?

**10  Make up your own poem about whales. Use this frame to help you.**

> Whales are good at _____
>
> Whales swim far out to _____
>
> Whales are _____
>
> I wish they would come play with me!

**11  Work in pairs to make up your own poem about seals. Your poem must have at least four lines and some words must rhyme. Write your poem on a sheet of paper and decorate it. Practise saying your poem aloud.**

Complete sentences; plan and write simple texts.

**12 Unscramble the sentences to write five facts about seals. Remember to use capital letters in your sentence.**

a) six are there of seal kinds found Antarctica. in
___

b) kind of seal crabeater one the is seal.
___

c) crabeater don't the crabs seal. eat
___

d) eat they krill.
___

e) icebergs. they on live
___

**13 Write your own sentences about whales. Use each word below in its own sentence.**

| biggest | Killer whales | krill | mammals |

## 14 Find and write the answers to these questions in your exercise book.

a) Which ocean surrounds Antarctica?

b) Is Antarctica bigger than our country?

c) What is an iceberg?

d) Name one difference between Antarctica and the Arctic.

e) Name three different kinds of animals that live in Antarctica.

f) If you lived in the Antarctic, what would you rather have: a layer of blubber or a warm jacket? Why?

## 15 Read the story about Herman the penguin chick's adventure.

Herman lived in Antarctica with his mother and his father. Herman's father, Mr King Penguin, loved swimming. In fact, he was very good at swimming indeed! Mr King Penguin decided to go hunting for food, so he stopped talking to his friends and dived into the sea.

Mrs King Penguin was nowhere to be seen, so Herman decided to go and look for her. He hoped to find her quickly because he was feeling rather scared and lonely. "My mother likes eating squid. Perhaps she's in the water with my father," said Herman to himself. "I shall go and find them."

Herman jumped into the water. It was so cold, but he kept looking for his mother and father. He enjoyed swimming in the water, but he still wanted to find his parents, so he decided to go back home to see if they were there. "Oh Herman, we have been so worried about you!" said his mother. "You agreed to stay home all the time. Why did you go swimming without us?"

"I wanted to be with you. I'm sorry. I promise to always ask you first before I swim," said Herman.

Find information and answer questions.

## 16  Answer the questions about the story

a) What was Mr King Penguin good at?

b) What did Mr King Penguin decide to do?

c) Why did Herman decide to go swimming?

d) Was this a good decision to make? Why?

e) Why must penguins be good at swimming?

f) Do penguins have to be good at walking? Why?

## 17  Write three reasons in each column.

| I'd like to live in Antarctica because ... | I'd not like to live in Antarctica because ... |
|---|---|
|  |  |
|  |  |
|  |  |

Answer questions; use 'because' to give reasons.

# Topic 6 Space

## Unit A The Solar System

1. **Play the 'Space rocks' game.**

   You will need a spinner and a different coloured counter for each player. Listen carefully to the rules of the game.

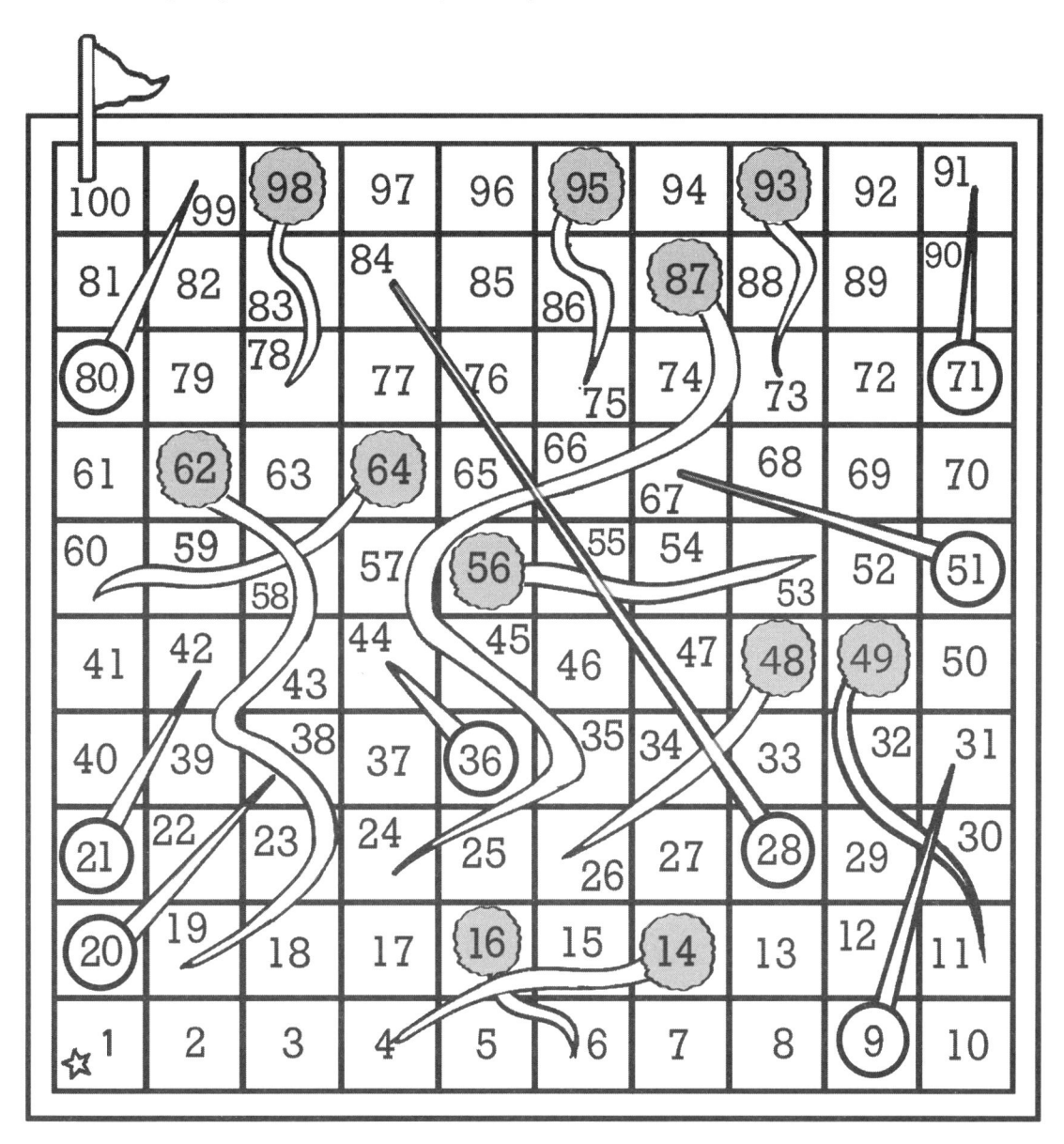

Listen and follow instructions.

**2** Work with a partner. Look at the picture. Ask each other questions about it.

**3** Complete this list of questions to ask the aliens. Choose question words from the box. You may use the words more than once.

| how | how many | how much | what | where | who |

a) _____ is your name?
b) _____ old are you?
c) _____ do you live?
d) _____ times have you been to Earth?
e) _____ planets have you visited?
f) _____ do you travel through space?
g) _____ do you like to eat?
h) _____ do you come from?
i) _____ would it cost to travel to your planet?

Use question words.

## 4 Lena and Marco are talking about their project. Circle the correct words so their conversation makes sense.

**Lena:** I am so excited. We are going to do (a / an) project on a planet. Let's do our project on Jupiter.

**Marco:** Do we have to do (the / that) project on Jupiter? Could we choose a different planet?

**Lena:** We could, but I have (many / some) information on Jupiter that we can use.

**Marco:** OK. Is (these / this) the information?

**Lena:** Yes, it is. Look at (this / these) pictures. Aren't they beautiful?

**Marco:** Yes, they are. I like (this / those) one more than (this / that) one.

**Lena:** Let's look for (some / many) more information.

**Marco:** I'll look through (the / these) books and you can look through (these / those).

**Lena:** I don't like (many / any) of the pictures in (these / this) book.

**Marco:** There are lots of good pictures in (this / these) book. (That / This) is a good book to use.

**Lena:** Let's make a poster (about / from) Jupiter.

**Marco:** OK, let's do (that / those).

## 5 Choose another planet. Write five facts about it.

1: _____

2: _____

3: _____

4: _____

5: _____

Use determiners; write factual sentences.

## 6 Read the sentences. Circle 'true' or 'false'.

a) Mercury is closer to the Sun than Earth is.   TRUE   FALSE
b) Venus has no atmosphere.   TRUE   FALSE
c) Pluto is a planet.   TRUE   FALSE
d) Mars is known as the 'Blue Planet'.   TRUE   FALSE
e) Asteroids are found on Earth.   TRUE   FALSE
f) Jupiter is the largest planet in our Solar System.   TRUE   FALSE
g) Earth is the only planet that has a moon.   TRUE   FALSE
h) Saturn has rings and moons.   TRUE   FALSE
i) The Great Red Spot on Jupiter is a storm.   TRUE   FALSE
j) The Voyager spacecraft found that Uranus has five moons.   TRUE   FALSE

## 7 Choose the correct ending for each sentence. Write it on the line.

a) We can't live on Jupiter because _____
   it is very stormy.   it is too big.

b) We can't live on Venus because _____
   it has an atmosphere of sulfuric acid.   it has no atmosphere.

c) We can't live on Mercury because _____
   it is too hot or too cold.   it is too flat.

Find information; use because to give reasons.

**8** **Fill in the missing words so the information makes sense. Choose words from the box.**

> aliens   asteroids   comets   meteorite   orbit
> Solar System   Sun   telescope   Voyager

Our _____ is made up of the Sun, planets and their moons. The _____ is actually a star. Planets are not the only things that move around our Sun. _____ are rocks that _____ around the Sun, along with planets. When an asteroid falls to Earth, it is called a _____. It is a good thing space is so big because _____ with tails of gas also travel across the sky. They are small and icy but their tails can be very, very long!

Some stars are so far away from Earth that we need a _____ to see them. Scientists sent a spacecraft called _____ to take photographs and find out more information about the planets. They found out a lot of new information about our Solar System. I wonder what the _____ thought when they saw a strange spacecraft flying through space?

**9** **Try this word puzzle. Make words with four or more letters. Each letter may be used once per word. Each word must have the letter E in it. List the words you make. Try to find at least one word with nine letters.**

| A | I | R |
|---|---|---|
| D | **E** | O |
| S | S | T |

Understand information; extend vocabulary and spelling skills.

**10  Write a recipe for a delicious alien meal.**

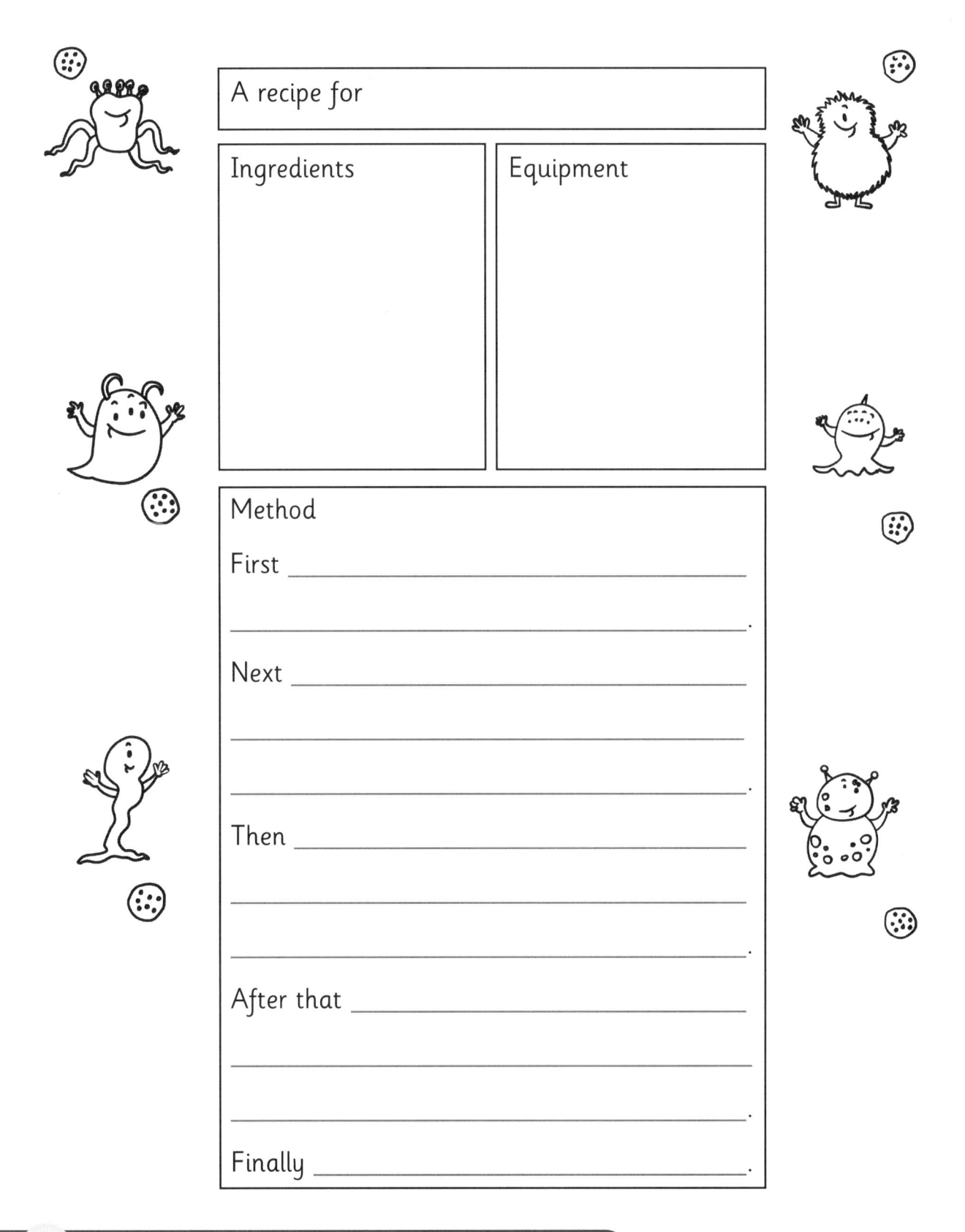

A recipe for _____

Ingredients

Equipment

Method

First _____
_____ .

Next _____
_____
_____ .

Then _____
_____
_____ .

After that _____
_____
_____ .

Finally _____ .

Use imperative forms; adverbs of sequence.

11  a) Label this diagram of the Solar System. Look at pages 34–35 of the Student's Book if you need to.

b) Write one fact about Neptune.

c) Write an opinion about travelling in space.

Find information; write facts and opinions.

# Unit B  Let's Go to Mars!

**1** **Listen to the words and their meanings. Tick each word as you hear its meaning.**

☐ travel     ☐ safety     ☐ spaceship    ☐ extra light
☐ strong     ☐ repair     ☐ space junk   ☐ entertainment
☐ weightless ☐ spacesuit  ☐ outdoors     ☐ orbit
☐ transfer   ☐ parachute

**2** **Find and circle the words in the word search. As you find each word, rewrite it below.**

| K | F | L | M | S | P | A | C | E | S | H | I | P |
|---|---|---|---|---|---|---|---|---|---|---|---|---|
| O | R | B | I | T | A | R | E | P | A | I | R | Q |
| P | W | G | S | A | F | E | T | Y | Z | H | R | S |
| A | C | W | E | I | G | H | T | L | E | S | S | P |
| R | I | E | X | T | R | A | L | I | G | H | T | A |
| A | S | P | A | C | E | J | U | N | K | S | G | C |
| C | T | R | A | N | S | F | E | R | T | S | U | E |
| H | X | N | P | Y | O | U | T | D | O | O | R | S |
| U | S | T | R | O | N | G | U | E | J | T | A | U |
| T | R | A | V | E | L | X | G | H | T | K | F | I |
| E | N | T | E | R | T | A | I | N | M | E | N | T |

_____   _____   _____   _____

_____   _____   _____   _____

_____   _____   _____   _____

_____   _____

Extend vocabulary and spelling skills.

**3** Read this letter from Fatima to her friend Rose telling her about her trip to Mars. Fill in the missing words. Choose from the box.

| best | colder | higher | largest | latest | longest |

Dear Rose,
I had a great trip to Mars. It was the _____ holiday of my life. It was also the _____ holiday of my life – nine months! I got to travel in comfort in the _____ spaceship! I saw the _____ volcano in the Solar System on Mars. It's three times _____ than Mount Everest! It was so much _____ on Mars than on Earth. I'm glad I had my warm spacesuit!
Your friend,
Fatima

**4** What would you tell a friend if you had just been on a trip to Mars? Write a short email telling about your trip.

To
From
Subject

Dear _____,
I'm just back from my very _____
The trip was so _____
The thing I liked most was _____
One thing that I really didn't like was _____
I am very glad that I _____
Your friend,
_____

Use comparative and superlative forms.

**5** Look at the page and read the information about Mars.

**6** Read what these children are saying. Tick the correct statements. Put a cross next to the incorrect statements.

☐ Mars is closer to the Sun than Earth.

☐ Mars is smaller than Earth.

☐ Mars is a ball of fire.

☐ Mars is much colder than your classroom.

☐ Mars is called the 'Blue Planet'.

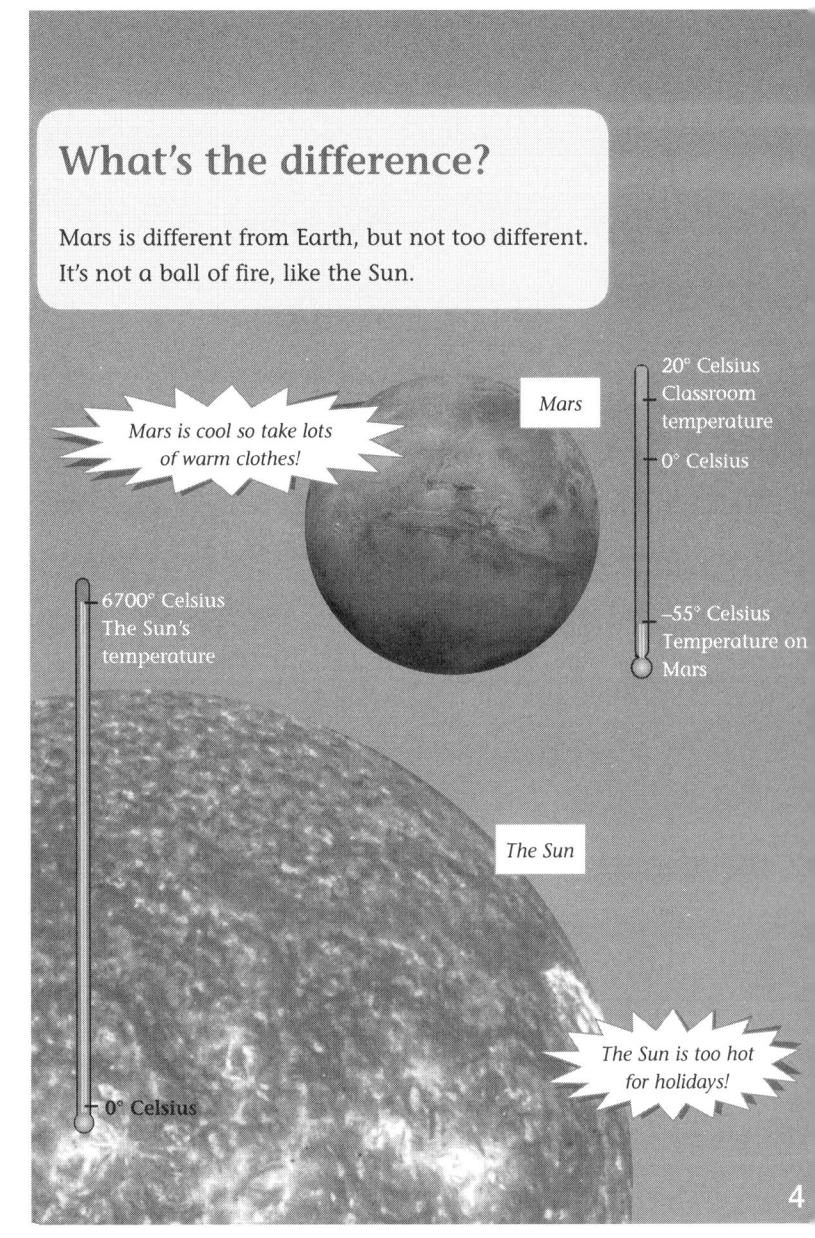

### What's the difference?

Mars is different from Earth, but not too different. It's not a ball of fire, like the Sun.

*Mars is cool so take lots of warm clothes!*

Mars

20° Celsius Classroom temperature
0° Celsius

−55° Celsius Temperature on Mars

6700° Celsius The Sun's temperature

The Sun

*The Sun is too hot for holidays!*

0° Celsius

**7** Write one true and one false statement of your own about Mars. Ask your partner to say which one is false.

_____

_____

88  Understand information and detail.

8  **Look at these diagrams. What do they tell you?**

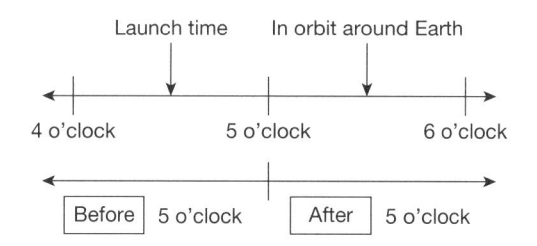

```
                Launch time    In orbit around Earth
                     ↓                ↓
    ←————————————————|————————————————|————————————→
      4 o'clock        5 o'clock        6 o'clock

              ←————————————————|————————————————→
               [Before] 5 o'clock  [After] 5 o'clock
```

The spaceship launched before 5 p.m. The spaceship orbited Earth after 5 p.m.

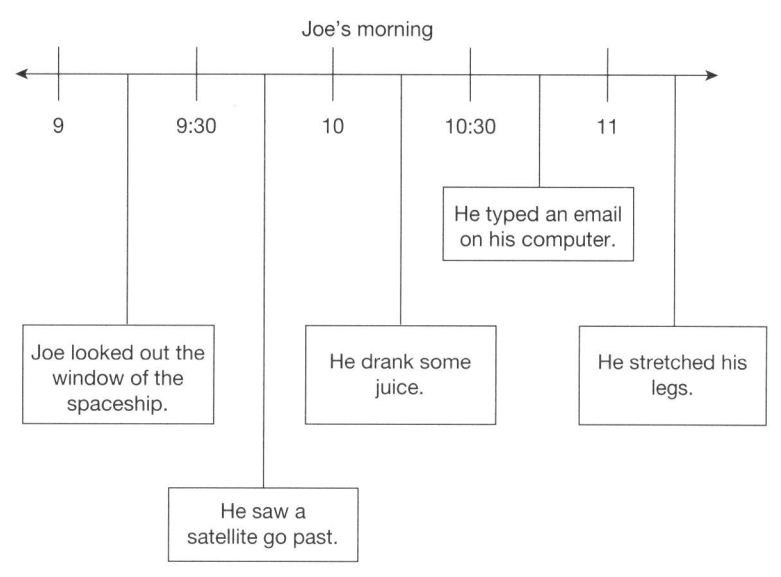

```
                         Joe's morning
    ←———|———|———|———|———|———→
        9  9:30  10  10:30  11
```

- Joe looked out the window of the spaceship. (9:30)
- He saw a satellite go past. (9:30)
- He drank some juice. (10)
- He typed an email on his computer. (10:30)
- He stretched his legs. (11)

9  **Write two sentences about Joe's morning using the word 'before' and two sentences using the word 'after'.**

_____

_____

_____

_____

Sequence information; use 'before/after'.

**10  Read and then answer the questions.
Tick the correct answers.**

a) How long does it take to get to Mars if you book tickets for the *Mars Express*?

Three days ☐     Three months ☐     Three years ☐

b) What might hit your spaceship when it is in the air?

An alien ☐     Space junk ☐     Another space ship ☐

c) What inflight entertainment will there be?

Weightless football ☐     Weightless tennis ☐

Weightless swimming ☐

**11  If people go to Mars they might be able to phone people on Earth.**

a) How long does it take for someone on Earth to hear you when you phone them from Mars?

b) These children are phoning their friends from Mars. Write what you think they are saying.

**12 Imagine you are going to visit Mars for a week. Complete the sentences about your plans for the week. Use 'going', 'hoping' or 'trying' in your sentences. The first one has been done as an example.**

The first thing we're <u>*going to do*</u> when we arrive is phone our parents.

On Monday, I'm planning to _____.

In the evening, I'm hoping to _____.

I'm _____ signs of life on Wednesday.

On Thursday, we _____ to have our photo taken with the Mars sign.

On Friday, my friends and I _____ to set a new _____.

I'm _____ pack my _____ on Saturday morning.

**13 There is a mistake in each sentence. Underline it and then rewrite the sentence correctly.**

a) I'm hope to arrive on Mars tomorrow.

_____

b) We are planning go to Mars next week.

_____

c) My spacesuit is arrive by special delivery tonight.

_____

d) We are have a farewell party at the weekend.

_____

e) Are you pack for the trip tonight?

_____

Express opinions; use persuasive language.

**14** **Write sentences about what you could do on Mars. Use the pictures to help you. Start each sentence with 'I could …'**

_____

_____

_____

_____

_____

**15** **Answer the question.**

> It will take the astronauts five months to reach Mars. The spaceship they travel in will be very cramped. They will not be able to shower with water and will only have tinned and freeze-dried food to eat. Would you like to travel to Mars? Say why or why not.

Use 'could'; express opinions.

# Unit C  Believe it or not!

**1  a) Look at the picture of Galileo standing next to his telescope. Write ten words that describe him.**

_____
_____
_____
_____
_____
_____
_____
_____
_____
_____

**b) Answer the question. Use some of the words you have listed.**

What was Galileo like?

I think he was _____

_____.

Write simple descriptions; use adjectives.

**2** **Use a pencil to mark all the missing punctuation marks and capital letters in these sentences. Rewrite the sentences correctly.**

a) neil armstrong walked on the moon

b) how many astronauts went to the moon

c) what an exciting adventure

d) the moon moves around earth

e) the hubble telescope has taken beautiful photographs

f) the astronaut said the sky is magnificent

g) the alien said take me to your leader

3   **What are you good at? Write three things.**

I am good at _____ , _____ and _____ .

4   **Reesha and her friends have decided to build a spaceship. Read what they said and then answer the questions.**

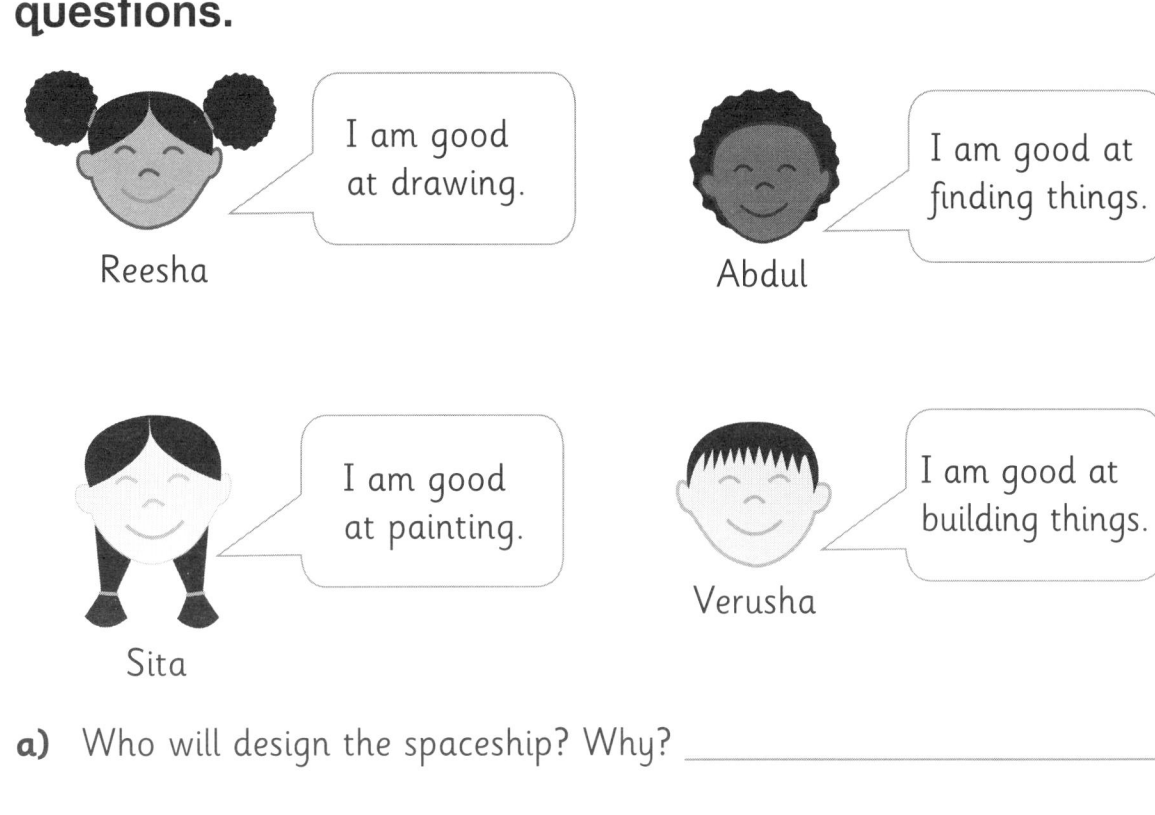

Reesha: I am good at drawing.

Abdul: I am good at finding things.

Sita: I am good at painting.

Verusha: I am good at building things.

a) Who will design the spaceship? Why? _____

b) Who will find the parts for the spaceship? Why? _____

c) Who will build the spaceship? Why? _____

d) Who will decorate the spaceship? Why? _____

Use 'good at'.

**5** **Choose an ending for each sentence from the box. Copy the ending to complete the sentences.**

a) Galileo wanted to see things that were far away, so _____ .

b) Galileo did not agree with the Church and _____ .

c) People did not agree with Galileo, so _____ .

d) The Church was not happy with Galileo, so _____ .

e) Galileo wrote about his discoveries, but _____ .

f) The Church decided that Galileo wasn't such a bad person and _____ .

> he said the planets moved around the Sun.
> he invented the telescope.
> they argued with him all the time.
> they put Galileo under house arrest.
> he went blind.
> they regretted treating Galileo so badly.

6  **Use words from the box to complete these sentences.**

| Earth | house arrest | ideas | moons |
| scientist | stars | Sun | telescope |

a) Galileo was a _____.

b) He liked to study the _____.

c) Scientists used to believe that the Solar System revolved around the _____.

d) Galileo believed that the Solar System revolved around the _____.

e) Galileo invented the _____.

f) He discovered that Jupiter has four _____.

g) Many people were upset with his _____.

h) Galileo was put under _____ _____.

**7** **What can you see in the picture? Tell your group.**

**8** **Write five sentences about the picture. Use the words in the box to help you. You may use more than one of the words in your sentences.**

> and   but   craters   Earth   flag   footprint   Houston
> moon landing   Neil Armstrong   or   orbit oxygen   planets
> Sea of Tranquility   spaceship   spacesuit

1: _____

2: _____

3: _____

4: _____

5: _____

Identify facts and opinions; use 'has/have' correctly.

9  **Read the sentences. Underline the opinion sentences. Tick the fact sentences.**

☐ The Moon is not a planet.
☐ Earth is a planet.
☐ The spacecraft landed on the Sea of Tranquility.
☐ Earth is the best planet in the Solar System.
☐ Mercury is better than Venus.
☐ The winds on Mercury are stronger than the winds on Earth.
☐ It is good to explore space.
☐ Aliens will take over Earth!

10 **Pretend that you are a newsreader. Read the story about the first Moon landing. Write 'has' or 'have' to complete the sentences.**

Men _____ walked on the Moon. The commander

_____ radioed to Earth. "Houston, Tranquility Base here.

The *Eagle* _____ landed," said Neil Armstrong.

The spacecraft _____ landed on the Moon. Neil Armstrong

_____ opened the hatch. He _____ planted the

first human footprint on the Moon. The crew _____

spent a total of two and a half hours on the Moon's surface.

The astronauts _____ become famous!

Plan and write short text. 99

# Topic 7 Storytime

## Unit A  Hector and the Cello

1  Read the speech bubbles. Fill in the missing words. Choose from 'that', 'this', 'these' and 'those'.

_____ guitar is mine.

_____ violin is his.

_____ instruments belong to us.

_____ drums are mine.

_____ drums belong to him.

_____ flutes belong to them.

2  Underline three sentences to show the things you would like to do most. Complete the last sentence to show one more thing you'd like to do.

I would like to play the cello.          I would like to play the drums.

I would like to sing in a band.          I would like to conduct an orchestra.

I would like to play the piano.          I would like to play the violin.

I would like to play the trumpet.       I would like to _____.

100  Use determiners; express likes.

3   **Number the pictures from 1 to 5 to match the order of the story.**

4   **Fill in the missing words.**

   a)   First Hector decided he wanted to play the _____.
   b)   Then Hector spoke to the _____.
   c)   Next he spoke to the _____.
   d)   Hector asked the lyrebird for _____.
   e)   Finally all the animals played in an _____.

Use adverbs of sequence.

**5  Complete these sentences. Use ideas from the box.**

| dark | dry | empty | fun | light | low | safe | wet |

a) The jungle is too wet. Let's go where _____.
b) The desert is too dry. Let's go where _____.
c) The room is too dark. Let's go where _____.
d) The bridge is too high. Let's go where _____.
e) The room is too crowded. Let's go where _____.
f) This place is boring. Let's go somewhere _____.
g) The room is too light. Let's go somewhere _____.
h) The jungle is too scary. Let's go somewhere _____.

**6  Write 'before' or 'after' to complete the sentences. One has been done for you.**

Hector wants to learn to play the cello. <u>Before</u> Hector can play the cello, he needs lessons. <u>After</u> he has lessons, Hector will be able to play the cello.

a) Hector needs money _____ he can have lessons.
b) _____ he has enough money, he will be able to pay for lessons.
c) _____ Hector speaks to the leopard, he speaks to the lion.
d) _____ he speaks to the leopard, Hector speaks to the rhino.
e) _____ he speaks to the rhino, he speaks to the snake.
f) _____ Hector has had lessons for two years, he plays the cello in a concert. Well done, Hector!

Complete sentences; use adverbs of sequence.

## 7 Write 'T' for true or 'F' for false.

a) The lion wanted to play the cello. _____

b) Hector tramped through the desert. _____

c) The other animals weren't very kind to Hector. _____

d) Hector picked up the rhino's spots. _____

e) Hector found a cello teacher. _____

f) Hector learned to play the cello, but he wasn't very good. _____

g) At the concert, the animals were surprised and happy. _____

h) They all played music together at the end of the story. _____

## 8 Answer these questions about *Hector and the Cello*. Underline the correct answer.

1. Why did Hector tramp through the jungle?

    a) He wanted to make new friends.

    b) He wanted to find a cello teacher.

    c) He wanted to meet the lyrebird.

2. Which animal hissed so much she slithered out of her skin?

    a) the snake

    b) the lion

    c) the rhino

3. For how long did Hector have lessons before the grand concert?

    a) two weeks

    b) two months

    c) two years

4. How did the lyrebird help the other animals?

    a) The lyrebird gave them all a cello.

    b) The lyrebird sent them all back to where they came from.

    c) The lyrebird gave them back the things that they had lost.

Answer questions; identify facts.

# Unit B  The Brave Baby

1 **Draw pictures to show the meaning of the words in the table.**

| big | bigger | the biggest |
|---|---|---|
| small | smaller | the smallest |
| tall | taller | the tallest |
| fluffy | fluffier | the fluffiest |
| short | shorter | the shortest |
| happy | happier | the happiest |

Use comparative and superlative forms.

**2  Read and follow the instructions.**

a) Circle the tallest tree.
b) Colour the widest tree.
c) Draw an arrow to show the thinnest trunk.
d) Underline the narrowest tree.
e) Tick the fattest trunk.
f) Write labels for each row to compare the three trees in that row. Choose a different thing to compare in each row.

**3** **Write a label for each picture. Complete the sentences using some of your labels.**

a) The Chief spoke to the _____.

b) Wasso played with a _____.

c) Wasso lived in a _____.

d) The wise woman spoke to _____.

e) The Chief danced for _____.

**4** **Write sentences to say what is happening in each picture. Write complete sentences. Use some of the words from the box.**

| afraid | blanket | brave | dancing | fierce |
| laughing | sitting | smiling | stick | |

**5** **Write sentences about the pictures. Use the example to help you.**

Example: The Chief was brave. He spoke to the wise woman.
          The Chief who was brave spoke to the wise woman.

**a)** The Chief was fierce. He spoke to the wise woman.
The Chief who _____.

**b)** The wise woman was old. She spoke to the Chief.
_____

**c)** Wasso was laughing. She sat on a blanket.
_____

**d)** Wasso was crying. She sat on a blanket.
_____

**e)** The Chief was tired. He slept in the wigwam.
_____

**f)** Wasso was happy. She fell asleep.
_____

**6** **Write three sentences of your own about the story.**

_____
_____
_____

Use defining relative clauses.

**7    Are the following statements true? Write 'yes' or 'no'.**

a)   The wigwams are near the trees. _____

b)   The big wigwam is behind the trees. _____

c)   The women are outside the big wigwam. _____

**8    Write five sentences describing where things are in this picture.**

at   above   below   behind
between   in   in front of
inside   near   next to   on
opposite   outside   to   under

108   Use prepositions.

9  **Look at the faces. Draw lines to match each face to a word that describes how the person is feeling.**

a)   b)   c)

sad    tired    happy    interested    surprised    angry

d)   e)   f)

10  **Read what the Chief wants someone to do.**

> I want the wise woman to fetch Wasso.
> I want Wasso to come to me.
> I want the villagers to dance with me.

a) What does the wise woman want? Complete these sentences.

I want the Chief to _____.

I want Wasso to _____.

I want the villagers to _____.

b) Write what you think these people are saying.

Use adjectives; use 'want to do'.

# Unit C  Hansel and Gretel

1. **Number the pictures from 1 to 6 to match the order in the story.**

[ ]    [ ]

[ ]    [ ]

[1]    [ ]

2. **Draw lines to match the beginning of each story sentence with its ending.**

How will we        •        • you the way home.

What will we       •        • eat?

We will see        •        • find our way home?

I will make        •        • you some food to eat.

I will show        •        • our father soon.

Sequence a story; complete sentences.

**3  Read the question. Tick the correct answer.**

a) Who told the woodcutter to take Hansel and Gretel into the wood and leave them?

☐ The old woman   ☐ The stepmother   ☐ The woodcutter

b) Who dropped crumbs behind him as he followed his father?

☐ The woodcutter   ☐ Hansel   ☐ Gretel

c) Who wanted to eat the children?

☐ A wolf   ☐ The old woman   ☐ The stepmother

d) Who was happy the see the children return home?

☐ The woodcutter   ☐ The stepmother   ☐ The old woman

**4  Listen. Do the words sound the same or different? Tick the correct box.**

|  |  | same | different |
|---|---|---|---|
| bird | hair | ☐ | ☐ |
| man | ran | ☐ | ☐ |
| walk | talk | ☐ | ☐ |
| forest | farm | ☐ | ☐ |
| stew | blue | ☐ | ☐ |
| owl | bird | ☐ | ☐ |

Answer questions; identify rhyming words.

**5  a) Find these words in the wordsearch. Tick the words as you find them.**

☐ gingerbread   ☐ stepmother   ☐ forest   ☐ stew
☐ Hansel   ☐ Gretel   ☐ hungry   ☐ picnic
☐ owl   ☐ path   ☐ cauldron   ☐ crumbs

| g | i | n | g | e | r | b | r | e | a | d |
|---|---|---|---|---|---|---|---|---|---|---|
| n | f | o | r | e | s | t | e | k | o | r |
| j | s | t | e | w | e | f | f | y | w | p |
| l | r | t | t | h | a | n | s | e | l | i |
| m | p | x | e | c | r | u | m | b | s | c |
| c | a | u | l | d | r | o | n | s | g | n |
| s | t | e | p | m | o | t | h | e | r | i |
| r | h | u | n | g | r | y | d | n | b | c |

**b) Which two words are proper nouns? Write them here.**

_____   _____

**c) The meanings of some words are given. Write the word next to its meaning.**

a large metal cooking pot: _____

a type of cake: _____

a bird with big eyes: _____

a place where there are lots of trees: _____

**d) What do these words mean?**

hungry: _____

crumbs: _____

Extend vocabulary.

## 6 Can you solve these riddles? Write your answers.

a) There are two of us. The woodcutter took us to the forest.
   We are _____.

b) I am big and black. I am round and I get very hot.
   I am a _____.

c) I fly silently. I can turn my head all the way round.
   I am an _____.

d) I am a person. I cut wood.
   I am the _____.

e) I am not young. I am not a man.
   I am an _____.

f) We are small. We come from bread. Birds eat us.
   We are _____.

## 7 Read the sentences. If the sentence is true, write 'T'. If the sentence is false, write 'F'.

a) The woodcutter took his children to the wood because he was cross with them. ____
b) Gretel heard her parents talking. ____
c) The stepmother went with them. ____
d) The children saw the old woman's house in the morning. ____
e) The old woman was making a stew. ____
f) Hansel heard the old woman talking to herself. ____
g) An owl showed the children the way home. ____
h) The stepmother was very happy to see the children. ____

## 8 Use each word in a sentence of your own.

| Gretel | Hansel | old woman | stepmother | woodcutter |

Extend vocabulary; understand detail; write sentences.

9  **Help Hansel and Gretel get home.**

Listen to the instructions. Play the game. The winner is the first person to reach home.

| 21 | 22 There's a tree in the path. Go back one block. | 23 | 24 | 25 *Home at last!* |
|---|---|---|---|---|
| 20 Stop for a drink. Miss a turn. | 19 | 18 Get stuck in some mud. Go down one block. | 17 | 16 |
| 11 | 12 You find a shortcut. Go up one block. | 13 | 14 Your feet are sore. Miss a turn. | 15 Build a bridge. Go up one block. |
| 10 Stop! There's a river. Go back one block. | 9 | 8 | 7 You find a clear path. Go forward four blocks. | 6 |
| 1 **Start** → | 2 Find a map. Go forward two blocks. | 3 | 4 | 5 You hear a noise! Wait here until you spin a 2. |

Listen and follow instructions.

**10 Write answers to the questions.**

What's the matter?

What's the matter with you?

What's the matter with your arm?

What's the matter?

**11 What would these children say if you asked "What is the matter?"**

Use 'what's the matter?'

12 **Write your own ending for each sentence.**

This is the man who _____.

This is the old woman who _____.

This is _____.

This is the house where _____.

This is the place where _____.

These are the birds which _____.

These are the crumbs which _____.

Use defining relative clauses.

**13  Think about the three stories in this topic.**

   **a)** Tick boxes to show your opinion of each story.
   **b)** Underline the name of the story you liked best.

| Title | I didn't enjoy the story | I enjoyed the story | I enjoyed the story very much! |
|---|---|---|---|
| *Hector and the Cello* | | | |
| *The Brave Baby* | | | |
| *Hansel and Gretel* | | | |

**14  Write a short review of the story you liked best. Use the frame below.**

Title: _____

The story was about _____

_____.

The bit I liked most was when _____

_____.

My favourite character is _____ because

_____

_____

_____.

I liked this story the most because _____

_____

_____

_____.

Express opinions; write a review with support.

# Topic 8 Interesting animals

## Unit A  Don't touch!

1   Where do these animals live? Tick the correct columns in the table.

| Animal | In the sea | In fresh water | On land |
|---|---|---|---|
| penguin | | | |
| shark | | | |
| rabbit | | | |
| frog | | | |
| bear | | | |
| seagull | | | |
| jellyfish | | | |
| tortoise | | | |

2   Find all the sea animals in this picture. Draw lines to match the names to the animals.

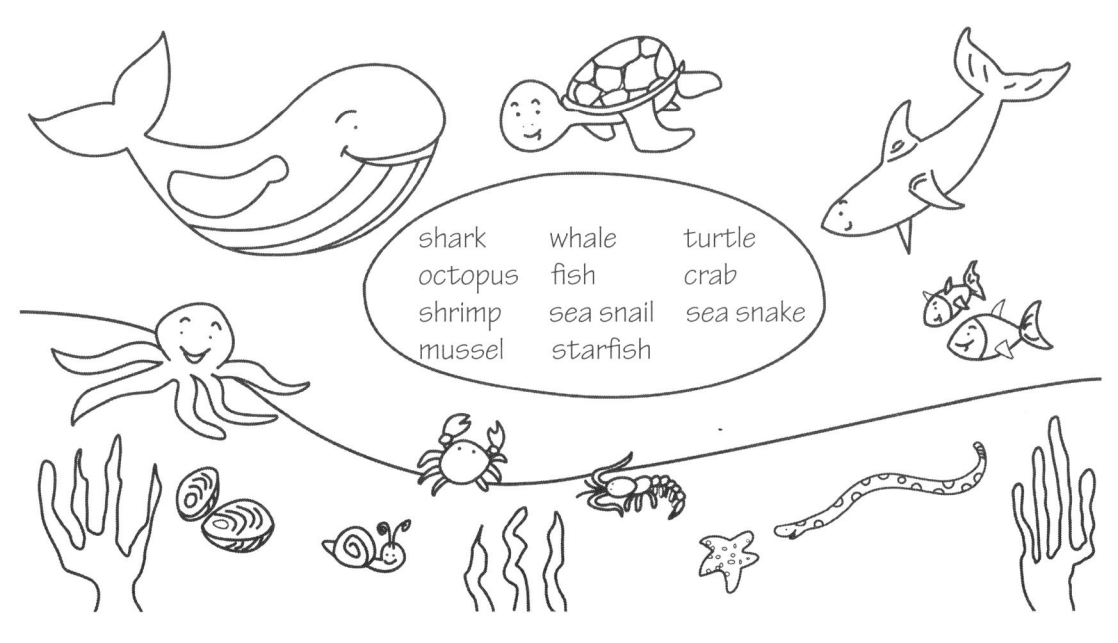

shark    whale    turtle
octopus  fish     crab
shrimp   sea snail  sea snake
mussel   starfish

118   Read for information; extend vocabulary.

3  **What do you think? Tick your answer.**

   a) Which animal do you think is the strangest?
      - [ ] octopus
      - [ ] triggerfish

   b) Which animal do you think is the most dangerous?
      - [ ] sting ray
      - [ ] jellyfish

   c) Which animal do you think has the best camouflage?
      - [ ] porcupine fish
      - [ ] sea snake

   d) Which animal do you think is scarier?
      - [ ] sting ray
      - [ ] shark

4  **Match the names to the animals.**

   jellyfish   porcupine fish   crab   sea snake   sting ray

5  **What type of animals are these? Label them. Spell the words correctly.**

   _____   _____   _____   _____

Use comparative forms; extend vocabulary and spelling skills.

## 6 Match the beginning of each sentence with its ending.

This triggerfish has • • because it is electric.

This crab has strong claws • • a sharp spine on its head.

This sting ray stays safe • • that cut and crush things.

The porcupine fish has spines • • their long tentacles that are poisonous.

These jellyfish can sting you with • • which can spike you.

## 7 Fill in the blanks with the correct word.

a) Sea animals look for _____ all the time.
   (food / spines)

b) The crab has strong _____.
   (claws / spines)

c) Some animals have found ways to stay _____.
   (hungry / safe)

d) The triggerfish has a _____ on its head.
   (spine / beak)

e) Jellyfish can sting you with their long _____.
   (tentacles / beaks)

## 8 Read the sentences. Write 'true' or 'false'.

a) The jellyfish has a hard shell. _____

b) The crab has strong claws that cut and crush things. _____

c) The sea snake has fins. _____

d) The octopus has eight legs. _____

e) The shark has lots of big teeth. _____

Understand information and detail.

**9  Choose the answer. Circle 'A' or 'B'.**

a) Which animal fills with water when it feels threatened?
   A   porcupine fish
   B   triggerfish

b) Which animal has a hard shell?
   A   starfish
   B   sea snail

c) Which animal has strong claws?
   A   shrimp
   B   crab

d) Which animal has long tentacles that can sting?
   A   jellyfish
   B   turtle

e) Which fish has a spine on its head?
   A   sting ray
   B   triggerfish

**10  Choose words from the box to complete the sentences.**

| strong claws | it is electric | a big spiky ball |
| ways to stay safe | spine on its head | |

a) Some animals have found _____.
b) The crab has _____ which can cut and crush things.
c) The sting ray stays safe because _____.
d) The triggerfish has a _____.
e) The porcupine fish fills with water and looks like _____.

Understand detail; descriptions.

11 **Read a learner's description of a shark. Write a short description of the other animals.**

| | | |
|---|---|---|
| | | |
| A shark is a sea animal with dark grey skin. A shark has triangle-shaped fins and sharp teeth. | | |

12 **What would you like to be? Circle 'would' or 'would not'. Give a reason why.**

a) I (would / would not) like to be a shark because _____.

b) I (would / would not) like to be a sea snake because _____.

c) I (would / would not) like to be a sting ray because _____.

d) I (would / would not) like to be a turtle because _____.

e) I (would / would not) like to be a starfish because _____.

Read and write descriptions; use 'because' to give reasons.

f) I (would / would not) like to be a sea snail because _____
_____.

g) I (would / would not) like to be a porcupine fish because _____
_____.

h) I (would / would not) like to be a sea urchin because _____
_____.

**13 Complete the table to show how each animal protects itself. Tick the boxes.**

| sea animal | spines | teeth | poison | claws | hiding |
|---|---|---|---|---|---|
| shark | | | | | |
| porcupine fish | | | | | |
| triggerfish | | | | | |
| sting ray | | | | | |
| sea snake | | | | | |
| jellyfish | | | | | |

Understand detail; summarise information.

# Unit B  Living dinosaurs

1  **Unscramble the letters. Write the words correctly.**

geg hoott _____ _____

sdraliz _____

noimtro rdzrila _____ _____

dicrescool _____

vgsecrsean _____

2  **Use the words from the box to label the parts of the crocodile.**

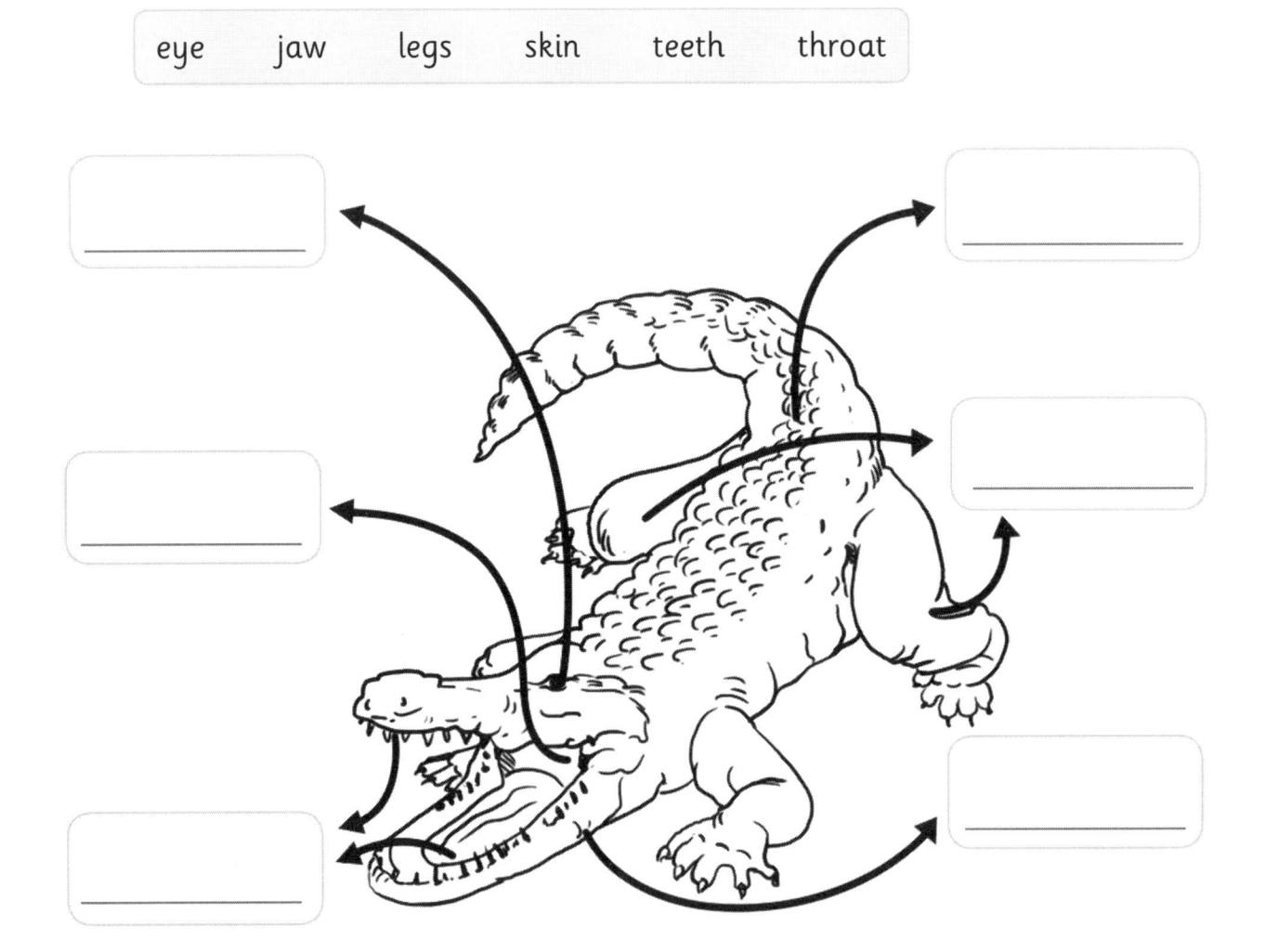

| eye | jaw | legs | skin | teeth | throat |

124  Extend vocabulary and spelling skills.

## 3  Find and circle all the action words in the box.

> attack   crush   dragon   egg   eye   grab   hunt   jaw
> legs   prey   skin   smash   swim   teeth   throat

## 4  Fill in the missing words. Use the example to help you.

<u>This</u> is a crocodile tail.

a) _____ crocodiles are hatching out of eggs.

b) _____ monitor lizard has a forked tongue.

c) _____ lizard is stealing a crocodile egg.

## 5  Fill in 'a', 'an' or 'the' to complete the sentences.

a) _____ crocodile has very sharp teeth.

b) Crocodiles have _____ flap of skin in their throats.

c) Monitor lizards have _____ egg tooth to help them break out of their eggs.

d) _____ monitor lizards steal crocodile eggs.

e) _____ monitor baby lizards often live in trees.

Identify verbs; use determiners.

# 6  Choose words from the box to complete the information below. Read it through to check that it makes sense.

> crocodiles   dinosaurs   egg tooth   flap   lizards   monitor lizards
> powerful   predators   scavengers   sneaking   underwater

Did you know that crocodiles and lizards have been living on Earth for millions of years? These creatures were living at the same time as the _____. Dinosaurs are extinct, but _____ and lizards are alive and well on our planet! We believe that they have survived for so long because they are such good hunters and _____ .

Crocodiles catch their prey by _____ up on an animal. They drag their prey _____ to drown it. Have you wondered why the crocodile doesn't drown as well? There is a _____ of skin inside their throats that closes – just another reason crocodiles have survived so long!

_____ _____ look a bit like crocodiles, but they are not related. In fact, the lizards try very hard to steal crocodile eggs to eat – they love eggs! Baby lizards use their special _____ _____ to crack their shells, but then they're on their own as their parents do not look after them!

7  Write a clear caption for each photograph.

a)

b)

c)

d)

Write simple captions (descriptive).

**8** Look at this index page from a book. Answer the questions about it.

## INDEX

alligators 11
crocodile,
 babies 12, 13
eggs 12, 13
farming 11
food 4, 5
hunting 3, 6, 7, 8
jaws 7, 10
kinds 11
size 9
teeth 6, 9
under water 8, 10

dinosaurs 2, 19
egg tooth 18
Komodo dragon 14
monitor lizard,
 babies 18, 19
food 16
hunting 3, 15
kinds 17
size 14, 17

**a)** Can you read about the size of crocodiles on page 9?

_____

**b)** Can you read about different kinds of crocodiles on page 10?

_____

**c)** Can you read about monitor lizard babies on page 18?

_____

128   Find information; answer questions.

9  **Look at the index page again and answer these questions.**

   a) What can you read about on page 3?
   _____

   b) What can you read about on page 13?
   _____

   c) What can you read about on page 6?
   _____

10 **What pages will you read to find the following information?**

   a) What is an alligator? _____

   b) What is a Komodo dragon? _____

   c) Where does a crocodile hunt? _____

   d) Does a monitor lizard eat fish? _____

   e) How many eggs does a crocodile lay? _____

   f) Does a baby crocodile use an egg tooth to break its egg?
   _____

   g) What does a monitor lizard eat? _____

Find information; answer questions.

**11 Skim read this information about monitor lizards to find information to complete the sentences.**

Monitor lizards look a bit like crocodiles but they are not related. The largest monitor lizards in the world are the Komodo dragons. They can grow up to three metres long and live for 20 to 40 years. They like to hide and then rush at their prey and bite it with their powerful jaws. Their mouths contain poison and even if their prey escapes, it will often die later from blood poisoning. Like crocodiles, monitor lizards are scavengers. They will eat anything they can find. They eat fish, dead animals, birds, frogs and other small animals. But they especially like eggs. They dig out crocodile eggs from the nest and eat them when the mother crocodile is away.

Monitor lizards look like crocodiles, but _____.

The largest lizards in the world are _____.

The Komodo dragons bite their prey with _____.

Their mouths are filled _____.

If their prey escapes, it will _____.

Monitor lizards will eat _____.

Monitor lizards eat crocodile eggs when _____.

Find information; answer questions.

## 12 Replace the words in brackets without changing the meaning of the text.

Female crocodiles lay their eggs on a sandy bank near the water and they stay near their eggs to keep (the eggs) _____ safe until they hatch. This takes about 90 days. When the baby crocodiles are ready to hatch out of the eggs, they make a squeaky sound to warn their mother to take care of (the baby crocodiles) _____.
They are now in great danger and many will be eaten by other animals, such as monitor lizards, before the female crocodile can carry (the baby crocodiles) _____ safely to the water.

Baby monitor lizards have a special egg tooth which they use to chip their way out of their eggs. Crocodiles have one too. Mother crocodiles look after their baby hatchlings, but baby monitor lizards have to look after (baby lizards) _____.

Baby monitor lizards often live in trees where they are safe from adult lizards who might eat (the baby lizards) _____. But like crocodiles, once they become adults, they are clever predators and scavengers, which is why these creatures have survived since the time of the dinosaurs.

Use pronouns.

**13** **The tables summarise the similarities and differences between crocodiles and monitor lizards.**

| Crocodiles |
| --- |
| live up to 80 years |
| up to seven metres long |
| have an egg tooth for chipping out of the egg |
| eat meat |
| eyes on top of their heads |
| powerful jaws and sharp teeth |
| look after their babies |
| powerful tail |

| Monitor lizards |
| --- |
| live up to 40 years |
| up to three metres long |
| have an egg tooth for chipping out of the egg |
| eat meat |
| eyes on either side of their heads |
| powerful jaws and sharp teeth |
| do not look after their babies |
| powerful tail |

To show differences, we can use the word 'but' in our sentences.

For example: Crocodiles can be seven metres long, but lizards are only three metres long.

We can use the word 'and' to show similarities.

For example: Crocodiles eat meat and so do lizards.

**a)** Write three sentences that show how crocodiles and monitor lizards are different. Use 'but' in each sentence.

1: _____

2: _____

3: _____

**b)** Write three sentences that show how crocodiles and monitor lizards are similar. Use 'and' in each sentence.

1: _____

2: _____

3: _____

Use 'and/but' for comparisons.

14 Write five facts about crocodiles. Use full sentences.

15 What do you think about crocodiles? Write a sentence giving your opinion.

16 Write five sentences about monitor lizards that are facts.

17 What do you think about monitor lizards? Write a sentence giving your opinion.

# Unit C  Big, bigger, the biggest

1. **What do you know about Africa? Complete these activities before you start this unit.**

   **a)** Complete these statements about Africa.

   I know _____.

   I know _____.

   I think _____.

   I think _____.

   I'd like to know more about _____.

   **b)** List the names of some African countries.

   _____  _____  _____  _____

   Can you find any of them on the map below?

   **c)** Tick the African animals in this list.

   ☐ rhino
   ☐ polar bear
   ☐ brown bear
   ☐ leopard
   ☐ lion
   ☐ walrus
   ☐ leopard
   ☐ kangaroo
   ☐ elephant
   ☐ tiger

   Use 'I think / I know'; extend vocabulary.

**2** **Circle the correct word in each statement. Use the pictures to help you.**

a) The elephant bull is (big / bigger / the biggest) animal in the picture.

b) The elephant calf is (small / smaller / the smallest) animal in the picture.

c) The elephant cow is (big / smaller / bigger) than the elephant bull.

d) Hippos are (smaller / smallest) than elephants and live on the banks of rivers and lakes.

e) Rhinos are also (smaller / bigger) than elephants but they can be as big as trucks.

f) Elephants are (bigger / the biggest) of the three.

Use comparative and superlative forms.

**3** **Use the words in the box to help you label the parts of the hippo.**

> feet    four webbed toes    grey-blue skin    huge head
> pink belly    short tail    two small eyes    two big nostrils
> short legs    two small ears    very big mouth

## 4 Read the information about rhinos. Highlight five important facts.

**Rhinos (or rhinoceroses)**

African rhinos have two horns on their noses. These are made of the same kind of material as our fingernails.

Rhinos have bad eyesight and they look clumsy. But few animals would dare to attack them. They have excellent hearing and they can be bad-tempered.

A rhino can run faster than a human. It can also dodge and turn very quickly.

Rhinos live alone or in very small groups. They are fully grown at five to seven years old. They can live for up to 40 years.

There are two kinds of African rhino: the white rhino and the black rhino.

The white rhino isn't white at all. It has a wide upper lip, so the word 'white' should really be 'wide'.

Rhinos usually have one baby, called a calf. Rhino mothers look after their calves for several years.

## 5 Write 'true' or 'false'. Correct the false statements.

a) African rhinos have two horns. _____

b) Rhinos have very good eyesight. _____

c) Rhinos are friendly animals. _____

d) Rhinos can run fast. _____

e) The white rhino isn't actually white in colour. _____

f) The white rhino should be called the 'wide rhino'. _____

g) Rhinos make very good house pets. _____

Find information; identify facts.

## 6  Follow the instructions to write your own folktale.

Step 1: Choose your main character.

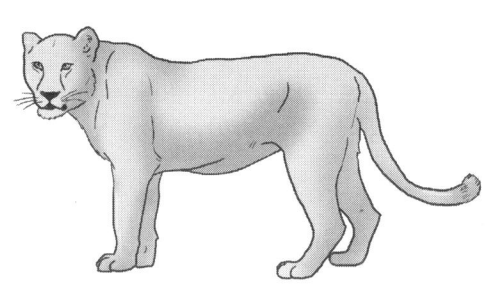

Step 2: Choose the setting for your story.

Step 3: Choose the problem for your story.
- Your character has lost something very special
- Your character is scared of his/her shadow
- Your character can't remember his/her name
- Your character is lonely and doesn't have any friends

Step 4: Brainstorm how to solve your character's problem. Write down your ideas. Then choose the best one.

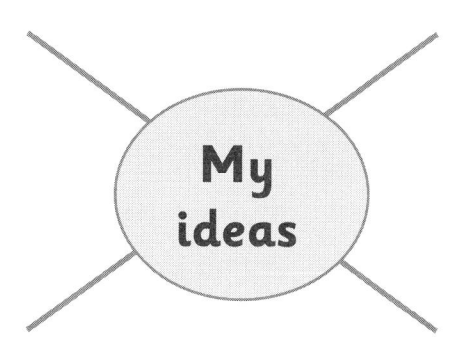

**My ideas**

Step 5: Start your first draft using this frame.

Once upon a time there was a _____ (main character) that lived _____ _____ (place). The _____ (main character) was very sad because _____ _____ _____.

The _____ (main character) decided that he/she was going to solve his/her problem, so he/she _____ _____ _____ _____.

Step 6: Finish your story and tell it to a friend.

Plan and write a story.

**7** **Choose words from the box to complete the sentences. There are different ways of doing this.**

| good | better | the best |
| bad | worse | the worst |
| much | more | the most |
| little | less | the least |

a) I think rhinos are _____ dangerous.

b) I think hippos are _____ dangerous than elephants.

c) I like elephants _____.

d) I like rhinos _____.

e) I think that poachers are _____ criminals.

**8** **Which wild animal do you like the most? Draw a picture of the animal. Write a sentence saying why you like it.**

Use comparative and superlative forms.

9  **Tick the boxes to summarise what you know about elephants, rhinos and hippos.**

| facts | elephants | rhinos | hippos |
|---|---|---|---|
| An adult can weigh 6,300 kg. | | | |
| Live on the banks of rivers and lakes. | | | |
| Smaller than an elephant but can be as big as a truck. | | | |
| These animals are killed for their tusks. | | | |
| These animals are killed for their horns. | | | |
| These animals are killed for meat and oil. | | | |
| Have bad eyesight. | | | |
| Have short legs and four webbed toes on each foot. | | | |
| Live alone or in small groups. | | | |
| Have a long trunk. | | | |

Understand detail and summarise information.

## 10 Read the clues and complete the crossword.

### Across

3   The name of a continent where elephants live.

6   Game wardens protect elephants, rhinos and hippos from these people.

### Down

1   Elephants, rhinos and hippos are three of the _____ animals on Earth.

2   Elephants, rhinos and hippos are called 'The Big _____'.

4   Poachers kill elephants for this.

5   A rhino can _____ and turn very quickly.

7   An African rhino has two of these on its nose.

# Topic 9  Let's explore

## Unit A  Marco Polo

1  **Tick the types of transport that Marco Polo could have used.**

☐ aeroplane    ☐ horse    ☐ elephant    ☐ bicycle

☐ ship    ☐ camel    ☐ train    ☐ 4 × 4 vehicle

2  **Fill in the missing words in the story. Choose from the box.**

> camels    China    crocodile    elephant    father    Gobi Desert
> goods    Kublai Khan    monkey    Silk    uncle    Venice    wealthy

Marco Polo travelled with his _____ and _____ to China. He saw many new places and animals on this journey. Marco Polo saw an _____ and a _____ and a _____. He also saw a rhinoceros. He thought the rhinoceros was a unicorn. It took many months to cross the _____ _____. Marco Polo learned about the _____ Road. He met many traders who were travelling all over the world to sell their _____.

Marco Polo became a special messenger for _____ _____. He was the emperor of _____ and he was very _____ and powerful. Marco Polo learned to speak Chinese so that he could speak to all the people. After 20 years, Marco Polo and his father and uncle decided to go back home to Venice. They did not travel back on _____. This time they sailed back home, but the journey was very dangerous and many people died on the trip. Marco Polo arrived back in _____ in 1295 CE.

Extend vocabulary; understand detail.

**3** **Marco Polo is telling his friends about his exciting adventure. Choose the correct word and complete each sentence.**

I _____ for China with my father and uncle. (leave / left)

We _____ many new places and animals. (seeing / saw / seen)

I _____ a rhinoceros was a unicorn! (thought / am thinking)

We _____ many interesting people as well. (meets / met)

Kublai Khan _____ me to be his special advisor. (tells / told)

I _____ all over China. (travelled / travelling)

I _____ how to make ice cream! (learned / learns)

We _____ to go home after 20 years. (decided / deciding)

It _____ a dangerous journey. (is / was)

I am _____ about my adventures. (writing / wrote)

**4** **What are they doing? Complete the sentences. Use the words in brackets to help you.**

a)

b)

Marco Polo is _____ a camel. (ride)

Marco Polo is _____ to Kublai Khan. (speak)

Use present continuous and past tense forms.

c)

Marco Polo is _____ to the trader. (talk)

The trader is _____ his goods. (sell)

d)

Marco Polo is _____ on a ship to Venice. (sail)

**5  Marco Polo wants to buy some things at the market. He is talking to the traders. Circle the correct word/s in each sentence.**

How (many / much) does the silk cost? (Where / Why) can I find more cloth? (How / Who) is going to sell me some spice? (Where / When) will you have more goods for me to see? How (many / much) jars of spice do you have?

**6  There is one word that doesn't belong in each set. Find it and cross it out.**

| Set A: | sea | ship | sail | ride |
| --- | --- | --- | --- | --- |
| Set B: | milk | ice cream | bread | pots |
| Set C: | pearls | diamonds | fireworks | rubies |
| Set D: | camel | horse | tiger | elephant |

Use common verbs; ask questions.   145

**7** **Imagine you are Marco Polo and you are being interviewed by a reporter. Answer these questions about your trip to China.**

**Reporter:** Why did you travel to China?

**Marco Polo:** I wanted to learn about new people and places.

**Reporter:** Why did you learn to speak Chinese?

**Marco Polo:** I wanted _____.

**Reporter:** Why did you speak to different people?

**Marco Polo:** I wanted _____.

**Reporter:** Why did you stay so long in China?

**Marco Polo:** _____.

**Reporter:** Why did you write a book?

**Marco Polo:** _____.

**8** **Try to work out the missing words in this puzzle. One is the name of a country, one is the name of a city and the third is the name of an explorer. Write the words in the correct places.**

# Unit B  Captain Scott

1  Can you work out which country each person is from? Use an atlas to check.

| | | |
|---|---|---|
| Our country is in Africa.<br>We come from K _ _ _ _ . | My country is in Europe.<br>I come from Aus _ _ _ _ . | I am Dutch.<br>I come from the Neth _ _ _ _ _ _ _ . |
| My country is in Asia.<br>I come from I _ _ _ _ . | I'm Irish.<br>I come from Ire _ _ _ _ . | The capital of my country is Seoul.<br>I come from South K _ _ _ _ . |
| Our country is next to the USA.<br>We are from Mex _ _ _ . | I am German.<br>I come from Ger _ _ _ _ _ . | The capital of my country is Tokyo.<br>I come from J _ _ _ _ . |

Extend vocabulary; use proper nouns.    147

**2** **Listen carefully. Tick the picture that matches each paragraph.**

Paragraph 1

Paragraph 2

Paragraph 3

Paragraph 4

**3** **Draw lines to match the punctuation marks to their names.**

, • capital letter

. • full stop

Q • question mark

! • speech marks

? • comma

" " • exclamation mark

**4** **Rewrite each sentence with the correct punctuation marks.**

**a)** my hands are icy cold said captain scott

**b)** can you see the camp asked james

**c)** help my hands are too numb to hold it shouted james

**d)** we need warm clothes hot drinks and a place to shelter

**e)** do you know the way he whispered

**f)** we should build a shelter don't you think asked james

**5  Use 'but' or 'so' to complete the sentences correctly.**

a) Scott had to get to Antarctica in summer, _____ the ship could reach land.

b) There are no trees in Antarctica, _____ Scott and his team brought a shed with them.

c) They built the shed, _____ it was not windproof.

d) The men needed to make the shed windproof, _____ they packed it with seaweed.

e) The men went on their journey, _____ it was difficult to travel.

f) It was very cold, _____ the men wore warm clothes.

g) Scott and his team reached the South Pole, _____ someone else had reached it first.

h) They could not stay there any longer, _____ the team returned to their home base.

**6  Complete these sentences.**

a) The men boiled water for tea and cocoa because _____.

b) Scott and his men were disappointed when they got to the South Pole because _____.

c) The two men set off, but they couldn't see where they were going because _____.

d) We know about what happened to Scott and his men because _____.

Use 'so', 'but', 'because'.

**7** **Work with a partner. Tell each other about the words in the box. Say what the items are used for.**

| | | | |
|---|---|---|---|
| blanket | diary | empty tin cans | gloves |
| leather bag | pen | tin mug | warm boots |

**8** **What can you see in Captain Scott's tent? Write five sentences about what you see. Use the words in the box to help you.**

I see a diary in the tent.

Extend vocabulary; write descriptions.

**9** **Read Captain Scott's diary entry.**

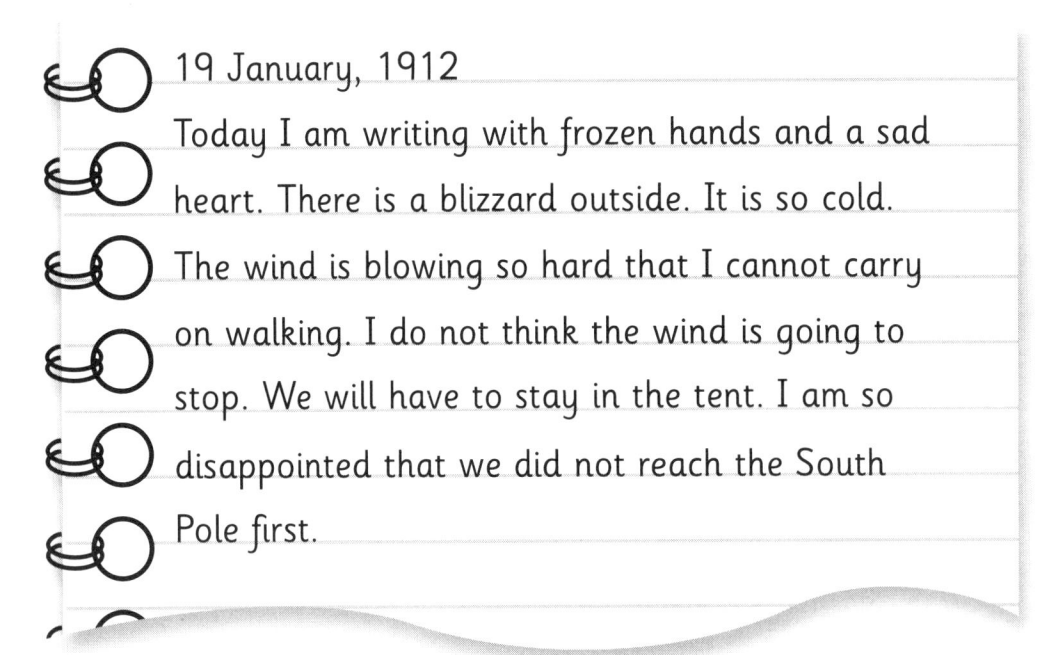

> 19 January, 1912
>
> Today I am writing with frozen hands and a sad heart. There is a blizzard outside. It is so cold. The wind is blowing so hard that I cannot carry on walking. I do not think the wind is going to stop. We will have to stay in the tent. I am so disappointed that we did not reach the South Pole first.

**10** **Imagine that you are on the expedition with Captain Scott. Write your own diary entry. Describe what you can see, what the weather is like and how you are feeling.**

> 15 January, 1912
>
> Today I

11 **Write 'true' or 'false'.**

   a) Captain Scott reached the South Pole. _____
   b) Captain Scott reached the South Pole first. _____
   c) It is always winter in Antarctica. _____
   d) It always feels like winter in Antarctica. _____

12 **Pretend to be Captain Scott. You are being interviewed by a reporter. Write the answers to the questions.**

   a) When did you leave Britain for Antarctica?
   _____

   b) What did you use to stop the wind and cold getting into the wooden hut?
   _____

   c) What was the date when you reached the South Pole?
   _____

   d) What did you drink to warm yourselves up?
   _____

   e) If the weather was good, how far could you walk each day?
   _____

   f) What did you find at the South Pole?
   _____

   g) How did you feel about this?
   _____

   h) If you could have the chance to do the trip again, what would you change?
   _____

Identify facts; answer questions.

13 **Imagine you are an explorer setting out on a journey. Write the answers to these questions. Use complete sentences.**

a) Where are you going to explore?

b) How are you going to get there?

c) What do you need to take with you?

d) Why do you want to explore there?

e) Draw a picture of yourself as an explorer.

# Unit C  Amelia Earhart

**1  Amelia Earhart had many interests. Listen to what she liked to do. Underline the activities that she liked to do.**

She liked to climb trees.

She liked cooking.

She worked as a doctor.

She liked to shoot rats.

She worked as a nursing assistant.

She was a telephone operator.

She wrote a book.

She ate a lot of cabbage.

Amelia Earhart was also a fashion designer.

**2  Rewrite each sentence with capital letters and full stops.**

a)  amelia earhart married george putnam in 1931

_____

b)  she was the first woman to fly across the atlantic ocean

_____

c)  fred noonan was her navigator

_____

d)  her plane went missing on her last trip

_____

e)  no one knows what happened to amelia earhart's plane

_____

Use past tense forms; insert punctuation marks.

## 3 Choose a word from the box to complete each sentence.

> aviator    brave    challenge    cockpit    disappeared
> famous    navigator    pioneer    sew    solo

a) Amelia Earhart was the only pilot in the plane.
   She was flying _____.

b) She liked to be the first person to do things. She was a _____.

c) An adventurer enjoys the _____ of going to new places.

d) A pilot sits in the _____ of an aeroplane.

e) Pioneers are very _____ people.

f) Amelia taught herself how to _____ her own clothes.

g) An _____ is someone who flies aeroplanes.

h) A _____ is someone who shows the pilot where to fly.

i) Lots of people knew about Amelia Earhart. She was very _____.

j) Amelia Earhart did not return from her last flight.
   Her plane _____.

## 4 Read the sentences below. Write 'fact' or 'opinion' next to each.

a) Amelia Earhart was born in 1897. _____

b) Amelia Earhart made really beautiful clothes. _____

c) Amelia Earhart should have stayed at home. _____

d) Amelia Earhart was a pioneer. _____

e) Pilots should be allowed to land wherever they want to.
   _____

f) Many people searched for Amelia Earhart's plane when it went missing. _____

g) The search cost too much money. _____

5. **Complete this missing person's report for Amelia Earhart. Draw a picture, and fill in the information you know about Amelia Earhart.**

   **Missing person's report**

   Name _____ _____

   When was she born? _____

   How old was she when she saw her first plane? _____

   Where was she last seen? _____

   Where was she flying to? _____

   Why was she doing this trip? _____

   _____

   _____

   Who is she with? _____

6. **Fill in the missing words. Choose words from the box.**

   | a | an | many | the |

   a) Amelia Earhart wanted to fly _____ plane around the world.
   b) She wanted _____ weather to be good.
   c) She was brave to fly _____ aeoplane on her own.
   d) Not _____ people would fly solo.

   Understand detail; write independently with support.

**7** **Cross out the incorrect word.**

**Amelia Earhart:** I want to fly (this / these) plane.

**Navigator:** Have you looked at (these / those) planes over there?

**Amelia Earhart:** I have, but (those / that) planes are too small.

**Navigator:** I like (that / this) plane in front of us.

**8** **Mark and Hans are doing a project on Amelia Earhart. They are talking about their information. Fill in the correct words. Choose from 'this', 'that', 'these' or 'those'.**

**Mark:** _____ project is fun!

**Hans:** Yes, I like doing _____.

**Mark:** I'm looking for some books.

**Hans:** There are some books on the shelf. Do you want _____.

**Mark:** No, I want _____.

**Hans:** Look at _____ picture of Amelia Earhart's plane.

**Mark:** Wow! I can't believe she flew _____!

**Hans:** She had to be brave to fly _____.

**Mark:** Here are facts about her trip. I'm going to write about _____.

**Hans:** I enjoy doing projects like _____.

**9** **Read the sentences about Amelia Earhart. Fill in the missing punctuation marks.**

a) Amelia Earhart loved flying

b) Have you ever flown a plane

c) Amelia said I want to fly across the Atlantic Ocean

Use determiners.

**d)** Would you like me to navigate for you asked Fred Noonan

**e)** Yes please replied Amelia Earhart

**f)** Where would you like to fly asked the navigator

**g)** I want to fly around the world she replied

**10 a) Write a statement about Amelia Earhart.**

_____

**b) Write a question about her navigator.**

_____

**11 Correct these sentences. Write out the correct sentences.**

**a)** Amelia earhart loved flying?

_____

**b)** She was A Wonderful woman

_____

**12 Write questions you would ask to learn more about Amelia Earhart's disappearance. Use the question words to help you.**

When _____

Who _____

Where _____

Has _____

Will _____

Did _____

Use punctuation correctly; use question words; write sentences.